The Tao of Dialo

CN00764925

Contemporary writers position 'dialogue' at the heart of change theory, but what do we mean by 'dialogue'? *The Tao of Dialogue* explains through story what dialogue means, and how to leverage dialogic principles in managing relationships within the workplace.

Accessible and innovative, *The Tao of Dialogue* explains the basic principles of dialogue, defined as a way of thinking and reflecting together with others, through the story of Michael, the CEO of a company about to embark on a life-changing journey. In the first half of the book, he is introduced to the idea of dialogue by Hannah, an internal change practitioner working within the organisation. He is encouraged to engage in dialogue with those he seeks to influence, which requires him to examine his mindset and proactively make changes to the ways in which he is communicating with his team and the wider organisation. In the second half of the book Michael is assisted by Mark, an external consultant with expertise in working with teams, who helps him apply dialogic principles to leading his team.

Emerging from dialogue between seven experienced, international coaches, *The Tao of Dialogue* will be of interest to coaches in practice and training, as well as business leaders, HR and L&D professionals and consultants. It explains in simple terms how to transform human relationships, both one-to-one and team/group. It will also appeal to academics and students of coaching, executive development, change management and leadership development.

Paul Lawrence is a lecturer in coaching at the Sydney Business School (University of Wollongong) and the owner of the Centre for Coaching in Organisations.

Sarah Hill is co-owner of Dialogix Ltd, specialising in behavioural change intervention combining structural dynamics and generative dialogue.

Andreas Priestland is a behavioural scientist and the owner and director of the Learning Project Ltd, a niche consultancy focused on leadership education, and organisational learning and change.

Cecilia Forrestal and **Monica Manning** work with the Community Action Network (CAN), a social justice NGO based in Dublin, Ireland.

Floris Rommerts is a trainer and coach based in the Netherlands.

Isla Hyslop is an organisational development professional who has been working in the UK public sector for more than 20 years, mostly in the NHS.

Routledge Focus on Mental Health

Routledge Focus on Mental Health presents short books on current topics, linking in with cutting-edge research and practice.

For a full list of titles in this series, please visit https://www.routledge.com/Routledge-Focus-on-Mental-Health/book-series/RFMH

The Tao of Dialogue

Paul Lawrence and Sarah Hill with Andreas Priestland, Cecilia Forrestal, Floris Rommerts, Isla Hyslop and Monica Manning

Routledge
Taylor & Francis Group

LONDON AND NEW YORK

First published 2019
by Routledge
2 Park Square, Milton Park, Abingdon, Oxon OX14 4RN

and by Routledge
52 Vanderbilt Avenue, New York, NY 10017

Routledge is an imprint of the Taylor & Francis Group, an informa business

© 2019 Paul Lawrence and Sarah Hill with Andreas Priestland, Cecilia
Forrestal, Floris Rommerts, Isla Hyslop and Monica Manning

The right of Paul Lawrence and Sarah Hill with Andreas Priestland, Cecilia Forrestal,
Floris Rommerts, Isla Hyslop and Monica Manning to be identified as authors
of this work has been asserted by them in accordance with sections 77 and 78
of the Copyright, Designs and Patents Act 1988.

British Library Cataloguing-in-Publication Data
A catalogue record for this book is available from the British Library

Library of Congress Cataloging-in-Publication Data
A catalog record has been requested for this book

ISBN: 978-0-367-07648-1 (hbk)
ISBN: 978-0-367-26614-1 (pbk)
ISBN: 978-0-429-02184-8 (ebk)

Typeset in Times New Roman
by Newgen Publishing UK

MIX
Paper from
responsible sources
FSC
www.fsc.org   FSC® C013985

Printed in the United Kingdom
by Henry Ling Limited

Contents

viii *Contents*

Acknowledgements

Seven of us wrote this book together and so we have lots of people we wish to acknowledge.

We'd like to acknowledge our family and friends, including Patrick, Ruth, Sally, Simon, Thomas, Joshua, Holly, Seonaid, Benjamin, Charlotte, Noel, Chloe, Callum, Fionn, Francis, Cameron, Ashleigh, Senan, Jeannie and Peter.

In addition, Sarah would like to appreciate the men and women living and working in prisons in the UK and the US where she first encountered dialogue of the kind we are exploring in this book. Monica and Cecilia would like to acknowledge everyone in CAN and all the people who sit with them in dialogue. Isla would like to thank all her friends and colleagues with whom she has been in dialogue, bringing their richness, teaching and learning to those conversations. Paul would like to acknowledge all the folks at CCO, and all the people he works with every day in Sydney and beyond, including the students at Sydney Business School and the Oxford Brookes 'tribe'. Andreas would like to appreciate the patience and understanding of all of those with whom he has conversed, as he has continued to learn. And Floris would like to dedicate the book to an emerging world of dialogic surfers.

And we'd like to acknowledge each other, and the experience of being together for three days at Beanacre.

Acknowledgements

Introduction

People use the word 'dialogue' all the time. They use it interchange-ably with words like 'conversation'. There is another, more specific, definition of 'dialogue', one that sits at the heart of communication and indeed the quality of human relationships. Dialogue, as defined by William Isaacs, is 'shared inquiry', a way of thinking and reflecting together. Dialogue, defined in this way, is conceptually simple yet diffi-cult to put into practice. There has been a lot written about dialogue. Yet the significance and practicalities of shared inquiry still appear to be poorly understood out there in organisations. We have written this book in an attempt to explain the basic principles of dialogue, and how those principles may be applied in an organisational setting. We have done our best to keep it simple and thereby accessible.

We used as a reference Max Landsberg's book *The Tao of Coaching*. The word 'Tao' has multiple meanings. Sometimes it is used to describe a path, or journey towards. Other times it is used to describe a way of being. In writing *The Tao of Coaching* Landsberg did a wonderful job in resisting the temptation to delve too deeply into theory, focusing instead on capturing the essence of coaching as defined at that time, and com-municating that essence in a form that everyone could understand. This book is our attempt to achieve the same with dialogue. It is not a defini-tive guide, far from it. It is our attempt to convey the essence of dialogue as we understand it – what it is, and how to begin working practically with dialogue as a leader, coach or consultant.

The Tao of Dialogue is the outcome of three days of dialogue that we engaged in together in a hotel in Beanacre, in the UK. We came together from the UK, the Netherlands, Ireland, Scotland and Australia. We didn't all know each other before we started, and we all work in different kinds of organisation. Lots of things emerged from the dialogue, most notably the model that underpins the second part of the book. We've called it the Beanacre Model.

Like Landsberg, we chose to frame our thinking around a story, drawn from our collective shared experiences of working in organisations. We have all worked with different kinds of organisations and had to choose one type for our story. In the end, we chose what some people would call a 'corporate'. Though the setting is corporate, we believe the content is relevant and applicable for other types of organisation too. For example, leaders and coaches working in the public sector and other not-for-profit organisations. If you don't agree, then let us know, and we'd be happy to write some different versions!

The first part of the book is told through the viewpoint of Michael, the leader of our fictional organisation, as he attempts to relate differently to people. The second part of the book is told through the viewpoint of Mark, a consultant, who helps Michael build a more effective team. Hannah also has a role to play throughout the story, guiding Michael on his journey. We hope the story will enhance your understanding of dialogue, and how to engage in dialogue in both individual and team interactions. Beyond the team there is a whole other book to be written about dialogue in the context of the whole organisation. But first things first.

Part I
Michael and Hannah

1   Contemplating change

In which Michael wonders how he will cope with a threat to his business

Michael put on his coat and headed for the elevators, wondering what on earth to do. Elaine, his Communications Director, had just told him the news. The Government had announced proposed changes to the law that, if implemented, would effectively wipe out one quarter of the business. The Government said the changes were necessary to encourage competition. They would certainly do that. New companies would be able to enter the market without any of the infrastructure that his company had invested heavily in over the last five years.

As Michael walked down the street he recalled the conversation with Elaine. The company would step up their lobbying efforts, she said, but he heard the tension in her voice. He had spoken to Nicole too, the Finance Director. She seemed less concerned. She said the company could cope. She had been with the company just nine months, arriving from another organisation where she had led a major downsizing programme. She told a great story about the programme at interview, but Michael had kept an eye on subsequent events and knew the organisation had recently been sold for a fraction of its original value. He wondered if she'd be useful or not. Tim, the Marketing Director, was initially downcast, but soon raised the subject of a new acquisition, a project he had been advocating for months without winning support from anyone else on the leadership team. He seemed oblivious to the bigger picture, focused only on his own agenda.

This company didn't do change well. The last time they embarked on a major change programme was three years previously. Michael had been Finance Director at the time, helping bed down the acquisition of a competitor business. The acquisition had been the old CEO's idea, and it hadn't gone well. Though the deal made sense on paper, neither their staff nor the staff of the purchased company ever really bought into the deal. People found it too hard to trust colleagues who had previously been competitors. Old tensions between certain staff members refused to go away and efforts to foster collaboration failed. Michael, along with the rest of the executive team, had worked hard to communicate the logic of the purchase, but to no avail. When key senior staff refused to comply with what was being asked, the CEO had asked four of them to leave, two from each side. They left, but not without taking other key staff with them. The relationship between members of the executive team fractured, and engagement levels across the organisation plummeted. More and more people left, and it was hard to attract replacements. In the end, the CEO and the Supply Chain Director were sacked, and the old Marketing Director soon followed.

Memories of those miserable days surfaced anew as Michael waited for his train to arrive. He couldn't go through all that again. But what to do? The company still hadn't recovered from those events of just 18 months ago. People still identified themselves with the companies they worked with before the acquisition. Trust levels were low and it was a daily challenge to get the right people round the table to make the decisions that needed to be made. This wasn't an organisation ready to align around a new future.

Elaine had already suggested they contract the services again of the consultants who had steered them through the last change. Michael couldn't think why. Nothing they had recommended had worked. No, he decided, as he found a seat on the train, they would need to do things very differently this time.

2 An introduction to dialogue

In which Michael meets Hannah, who advocates a different approach to change

By the end of the week rumours about the impending changes had begun to circulate around head office and out into the regional offices. Elaine told Michael she thought he needed to gather all the staff together – to hold a Town Hall meeting. People were getting anxious, she said, anxieties that needed to be managed if they weren't to disrupt ongoing business. Some people were saying that the company was already planning redundancies. She drafted up a short speech for him and prepared a list of anticipated questions and answers. Elaine's suggestion made sense, and the rest of the leadership team also encouraged him to stand up and tell everyone what was going on. Rather than leave people to stew over the weekend, Michael decided to call an impromptu gathering late on Friday afternoon.

'Good afternoon, everyone,' he began, looking out into a room full of people. 'By now you will have heard that the Government is floating new laws that will have a significant impact on our business.'

Everyone sat silent, staring at him, some with arms folded. Michael saw Elaine at the back of the room standing straight backed and sombre. She nodded slightly, encouraging him to continue.

'It's important we recognise these are currently just proposals,' Michael continued. 'It will be many months before we find out what will actually happen. In that time, we will be putting our case to government, arguing against new laws that will only lead to job losses and disruption. While this all plays out we must work even harder to cement our position in the marketplace. It is up to us *all* to pull together and do what needs to be done.'

It was a short speech. While he hadn't expected applause, he was surprised that no one spoke.

'Any questions?' he said, pulling from his pocket Elaine's list of questions and answers. He had memorised them at lunchtime, but it helped to hold the list in his hand.

A hand went up. 'Will there be any redundancies?' someone asked.

'We have no plans to make people redundant,' Michael answered.

'But what if these new laws go through, will there be redundancies then?'

Michael shook his head. 'It's too early to be thinking about redundancies,' he said. 'For one thing, it's unlikely these proposals will go through as currently framed. There will be some kind of review process. We will review our strategy as the process unfolds and make decisions in due course.'

A hand went up somewhere in the middle of the room. Michael nodded.

'If the new laws go through, I've heard we may lose up to a third of our business,' said someone Michael couldn't see. 'What strategies are there for making that up?'

Michael nodded again. 'First, we doubt the impact will be quite that significant,' he said. 'But clearly we may need to move faster than planned to identify new growth opportunities. Again, that will be up to us all to make that happen.'

A few people muttered quietly, but no one else asked a question. Michael looked at the clock and saw it was almost five o'clock. 'Thank you all for your time today,' he said. 'If anyone would like to stay behind for a while, we will be serving drinks.' He pointed to the back of the room where bottles of wine and beer sat on a table next to some glasses.

There was a shuffling of chairs and a low rumble of conversation as people drifted slowly out of the room, leaving a couple of dozen behind with whom to mingle. Elaine strode forward and patted him on the back.

'Good job,' she said. 'Clear and unambiguous.' Nicole and Tim congratulated him too, before moving away to talk to staff in their respective divisions.

Feeling somewhat relieved, Michael helped himself to a glass of white wine, rubbing shoulders with someone he recognised from the HR team. Sharon? Or Sheryn? He couldn't quite recall. He smiled. 'What did you think of that?' he asked.

She shrugged her shoulders and smiled hesitantly. 'It depends on what you were hoping to achieve.'

'What do you mean?' Michael asked, surprised.

'A Town Hall is a Town Hall,' she said. 'As Town Halls go, I thought it was fine.'

'You work in HR, don't you?' Michael asked, curious.

'I do,' she replied. 'I'm Hannah by the way.'

'Right,' Michael said, nodding. Not Sharon, then.

'Do you mind if I give you a bit of feedback?' she said, cheeks burning red. 'It's not really my place to say, but I wouldn't have held a Town Hall at all.'

'Oh,' said Michael, feeling slightly put out. 'What would you have done?'

'I would have gone for a more dialogic approach,' said Hannah. 'In smaller groups. A Town Hall is essentially monologic. No one has a chance to ask questions, not real questions, or to engage with you in real dialogue. It was you, basically, telling them what you thought they wanted to hear. But I'm afraid you may have missed the mark.' She waved an arm at the almost empty room. Michael noticed that the rest of the leadership team had gone.

'I don't know what you mean,' Michael said. 'What's dialogic and monologic?'

'Ah,' said Hannah, before taking the time to explain. By the time she had finished Michael had drunk a second glass of wine and gotten a glimpse of what needed to happen next.

Monologue and dialogue

Before and during every conversation we make a choice (consciously or otherwise) as to what type of conversation we want to have. Do we want to engage in monologue or dialogue? There is no right or wrong choice, but there *is* a choice. The choice is whether to *defend* or *suspend*.

If I choose to *defend*, then I choose to protect and uphold a particular position or perspective. In Michael's case, for example, he chose to defend a perspective that said, *'we're not going to talk about options today – there will be a review process later.'* In contrast, if I choose to *suspend*, then I am more open. Had Michael suspended his position and view, he would have been more likely to respond to a question like *'What strategies are there for making that up?'* with a response such as *'We don't have any yet, but I'd be keen to hear what you think.'* In dialogue participants are open to new possibilities. Contributions build upon contributions, and new insights emerge. By choosing to *defend*, Michael inadvertently narrowed the range of possible outcomes. People didn't feel their views would be welcomed and chose not to engage.

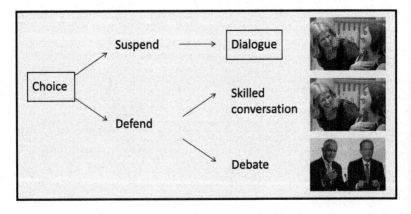

Figure 1 Dialogue and monologue (after Isaacs, 1999)

Most of us readily identify *debate* as a form of monologue, people tossing opinions at each other without any intention of changing their mind. *Skilled conversation* is more difficult to differentiate from dialogue. They often look the same (which is why we have used the same pictures for each in Figure 1). If two people come to a conversation, respecting each other's 'non-negotiables', the ensuing conversation may be both productive and useful. It is still however, likely to be convergent. What emerges is a (skilfully) negotiated outcome. Nothing new is likely to emerge.

There are many situations that call for debate and/or skilled conversation. To engage others in the creation of new possibilities however, to engage others in change, necessitates some form of dialogue. As Michael is about to discover, engaging in dialogue is not as easy as many of us think.

3 How dialogue works

In which Michael does meaning making

On Monday morning Michael invited Hannah out for a coffee. He let Elaine know first, since Hannah reported to Elaine. Elaine looked puzzled but raised no objections. Michael agreed to meet Hannah at a coffee shop just a five-minute walk from the office. When he arrived, she sat at a table waiting for him.

'So,' Michael said, 'If I understood you right on Friday, you were saying that by engaging people in a Town Hall format I wasn't giving people the opportunity to say what they really thought.'

'That's right,' said Hannah. 'I thought you did well to get any questions at all, but no one was going to say what they really thought because it wasn't a safe environment in which to speak up.'

'What do you mean, "it wasn't a safe environment"?'

'Come on. You're the CEO,' said Hannah. She is very assertive, thought Michael. 'In this organisation, like most organisations, you don't challenge your superiors in a public forum; they don't like it,' she said. 'That's what we call a "career limiting move!"' She sipped her coffee and shook her head. 'And you had virtually the whole of the executive team standing at the back of the room watching. That's what I mean by not safe.'

'*You* told me what you think,' said Michael.

'I told you in private and I'm thinking of leaving. I wouldn't have spoken up otherwise.'

'Well that's disappointing,' said Michael. He made a mental note to talk to Elaine about incentivising Hannah to stay. 'How do we know what people are thinking if they won't speak up?'

Hannah smiled. 'If you want people to speak up then you have to be genuinely interested in what they have to say.'

'I am genuinely interested!' Michael protested.

'It didn't seem like it,' said Hannah. 'Think about it. First, you gathered everyone in a big group under the watchful eyes of the leadership team with you towering over them at the front. That says to everyone – hear what we have to say and make sure you do as we ask.'

Really? – thought Michael. Didn't feel like I was towering.

'Second, you told us absolutely nothing that we didn't know already. You told us the Government are thinking about making changes to the law. We knew that. You told us you're going to be lobbying them. Not hard to guess. You told us you don't currently have plans to make people redundant. No surprise there – everyone knows it takes the executive team ages to make big decisions. You told us you'll be reviewing strategy.' She pulled a face.

'That's all there is to know,' said Michael.

'Hardly,' said Hannah, sipping at her coffee. 'You could have told us what you're thinking. What some of the scenarios might be. Just shared some of your thoughts and feelings.'

'But what good would that have done?' said Michael. 'That would just have got people even more anxious.'

Hannah shook her head. 'You made them more anxious by telling them nothing. Now they know you're not going to tell them anything unless you have to. Now they know you don't trust them to respond reasonably if you tell them something tough to hear.'

'Tell people the facts and don't feed the rumour machine,' said Michael, sitting up straight. 'That's what I've learned.'

'The rumour machine feeds itself,' said Hannah. 'People don't just take what you tell them and swallow it whole. Everyone there on Friday went off to the pub, or went home to their partners, or else are sitting in cafés now, just like us, making sense for themselves of what they're reading in the papers, what you said on Friday, and what their managers told them this morning. They will make meaning of what's going on, *for themselves*. All you can do is hope to influence that meaning making process, by engaging in dialogue. As it is, you've chosen not to engage in that process. You're absenting yourself from the conversation, thereby *giving* up the opportunity to influence. To influence effectively you must adopt a dialogic mindset.'

Michael scratched his head and studied Hannah's flushed face. Even though she was thinking of leaving, she had still taken a big risk choosing to lecture him like this. How refreshing. He was sick and tired of people blindly agreeing with everything he said. He had no idea what a 'dialogic mindset' was but decided to find out.

'If I clear it with Elaine, will you work for me a couple of days a week?' he asked. 'I think I'm going to need to talk to you on a fairly regular basis.'

'I'll resign my role and work for you on contract, as long as Elaine is OK with it,' Hannah replied.

'OK then,' said Michael, again surprised. 'Let me get back to you.'

A dialogic mindset

Hannah is prone to using jargon. She's particularly fond of the phrase 'dialogic mindset'. What she's getting at is the idea that engaging in dialogue is less of a skillset or toolkit and more a way of being. It requires a particular mindset, based on a belief in the idea that we make meaning *for* ourselves, but not *by* ourselves.

Think of the people who attended Michael's Town Hall. They didn't process what they heard like robots. They all had questions, a few of which got expressed. But Michael didn't seem interested in exploring those questions and so everyone headed off to the nearest café/pub to make sense of what they heard – together. And what emerged from those conversations will determine what sense they make of Michael's speech, and how they will behave moving forward.

A 'dialogic mindset' acknowledges that this is how human beings function. We can compare the dialogic mindset to the monologic mindset (see Table 1).

Relating to the world through a dialogic mindset, I see myself as one player on the stage among many. I notice that everyone has different experiences, beliefs and values, and is standing in a different position. Where I am standing, determines my perspective. I can see my perspective is not the only perspective and I am curious to understand the world through other's eyes.

Table 1 Dialogic and monologic mindsets

Dialogic mindset	Monologic mindset
Seeks to understand	Seeks agreement
Speaks to 'offer'	Speaks to 'demand'
Focuses on listening and speaking	Focuses mostly on speaking
Is open to new possibilities	Is committed to pre-determined outcomes
Leads to shared meaning	Leads to clashes in meaning
Embraces uncertainty	Commits to certainty

4 Listening

In which Michael experiments with different ways of listening

Next day Michael and Hannah met again. Michael began by asking her if she was prepared to act as a sounding board, keeping the content of all their conversations confidential. Hannah agreed. Michael nodded, before telling her about what happened at a recent board meeting.

At the meeting, one particular member of the Board, David, seemed intent on pushing forward Tim's investment idea. Michael told Hannah he almost lost his temper with David. The tension between them was evident to everyone else at the meeting.

'Tell me what you heard,' said Hannah.

'I heard what he said,' Michael replied, getting cross. 'He said we needed to acquire a local player in the Eastern European market. He said we couldn't hope to grow a business from scratch because we don't understand how the market works.'

'What did you say?'

'I said it's precisely because we don't understand the market that we don't have the know-how to buy someone. Second, we don't have a great track record in acquiring other businesses. We're still trying to fix the last mess we created.'

'OK,' said Hannah. 'So, you were in monologue again.'

'What do you mean?'

'I mean you went into the conversation unwilling to listen to anything that went against your list of non-negotiables. One of your non-negotiables is "no acquisitions".'

'Well?' Michael replied. 'That *is* a non-negotiable for me.'

'Which got in the way of your listening. You were locked in to listening for *content*, and oblivious to both *intention* and *identity*.'

'Explain?'

'When we listen for *content*, we're listening only to the words someone uses. We don't stop to question whether what we're hearing is what the speaker is trying to say. We take the word and attach our meaning to it, *assuming* we understand what is being said.'

'As opposed to?'

'Listening for *intention*, where we are focused on what other people are *trying* to say. If I'm listening for intention, I don't jump in straight away with my viewpoint. I check-in, make sure I've really understood what the other person intends to say. And listening for *identity* is where I'm seeking to understand not just what the other person is trying to say, but why. It's about listening out for that person's experiences, values, and deep-seated beliefs. I've got a much better chance of establishing a good relationship with someone if I know who they are.'

'So, what do you suggest I do?'

'I suggest you go talk to him and experiment with different ways of listening.'

Two days later, Michael met again with Hannah. The conversation with David had gone better than expected. It appeared that David wasn't wedded to the idea of a traditional acquisition. What was important to David was that the company established some kind of foothold in the new market. As they talked, Michael had realised that he and David had a lot in common. David wasn't particularly keen on traditional acquisitions either. As Michael poked and prodded David, seeking to understand where he was really coming from, the idea of a strategic alliance emerged. A strategic alliance wouldn't be easy to make happen either, but it was a better option than acquisition.

As Michael reflected on the conversation with David, he realised how much better he now understood him. From David's previous experiences working for a capital management consultancy, he had a strong belief in the value of relationships and partnerships in leveraging full value from any kind of commercial enterprise. He had become frustrated with Michael at the original board meeting because Michael didn't seem to want to work with him. Michael felt chastened, reflecting upon the way he had behaved with David. He resolved not to fly off the handle so easily. In future, he decided, he would do a lot more of this 'listening for intention' and 'listening for identity'.

Listening model

It's all very well going into a conversation with the intention of 'suspending' our point of view but it's easier said than done. The listening model provides us with practical guidance as to how we might listen differently.

Sometimes we go to meetings, or just show up in conversations, biding our time, waiting for the opportunity to make a point. Our inner voice is loud, blocking out anything others are saying. The inner voice says things like '*When will he/she stop talking*', and when the noise stops, and I have the chance to speak, I am likely to leap in with something like '*Can I just say something …*'. We call this *listening for noise*, a monologic listening style. At times it may be appropriate, for example when there is a crisis, and I absolutely have to get my point across and make sure others hear what I have to say, quickly. Often, it's not appropriate.

Other times I am *listening for content*. I am listening to every word. I can recite back to you exactly what you said. But I am unwittingly making assumptions, leaping to conclusions, adding *my* meaning to *your* words. For example, you tell me I could be a better communicator. What you are trying to tell me is that I need to speak out louder, more often. I hear what you say and focus on listening more and speaking less, because I define 'communication' differently. I have listened to your words, but haven't understood what you were trying to say. This form of listening is also appropriate sometimes, when again we need to get things done quickly, the scenario is low risk, and/or I'm confident we speak the same language. Again though, it is a monologic listening style.

If I make a special effort to understand what you are *trying* to say, then I am *listening for your intention*. If I'm listening in this way I will hear myself paraphrasing, checking in regularly to make sure I understand what you're trying to tell me. '*So, you're telling me I need to focus more on listening?*' I give you the opportunity to correct me, to help me understand your true intent. This is a more dialogic way of listening, required when it is important for people to understand each

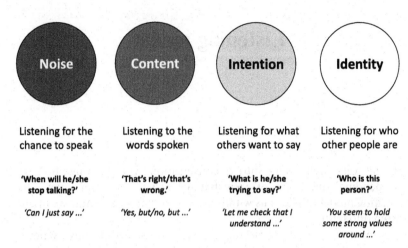

Figure 2 Listening model

other. Finally, sometimes, I want to understand not only what you are trying to say, but *why* you are trying to say it. What is it about you, that you value speaking over listening? I'm *listening for identity*, a form of listening that helps me truly understand you and helps me understand how best to relate with you moving forward.

5 Listening again

In which Michael discovers there's more to listening than the listening model

Encouraged by his recent conversations with David, Michael decided to talk to Nicole, the Finance Director. He had heard through Tim that Finance were already working on cost reduction scenarios, and that one or two people in Finance were discussing these scenarios openly with others in the organisation. Michael was angry. The executive team had not had any kind of conversation about cost reduction, but no one else knew that. If more people heard was what going on, they might assume that the executive team were already planning redundancies, despite what he'd said at the Town Hall. Michael went to see Nicole, determined to put the listening model into practice. This is how he recounted the conversation to Hannah:

MICHAEL: Nicole, I've heard that you're running some redundancy scenarios. Is that right?

NICOLE: We're running some cost reduction scenarios, of course. Whatever happens, we're almost certainly going to have to cut costs somewhere, so we need to be ready.

MICHAEL: So that *is* what's going on? You are running cost reduction scenarios?

NICOLE: That's our job, Michael.

MICHAEL: It's your job to think through redundancy scenarios, without telling me or anyone else on the executive team? It didn't occur to you that people on your team might share some of that work with people outside Finance, and that the organisation might assume you're doing it on behalf of all of us?

NICOLE: No one should be sharing any of that work with people outside Finance.

MICHAEL: But they are, apparently. I'm getting the sense Nicole, that you like to work quite autonomously, and that you don't believe in being careful about what gets said and what doesn't.

NICOLE: How did you come to those conclusions?

MICHAEL: First, you've gone ahead and done this work without telling anyone. Second, you didn't seem too concerned by the news last week. I can only connect that with what's happened at the last organisation you worked for. You said you played a leading role in implementing their change programme and look what's happened there.

NICOLE: Wow! Well let me respond, Michael. First, as I said, it's my job to work through these scenarios, confidentially of course. If someone's been speaking out of turn then I'd like to know who. Second, I'm as worried by the news as anyone. That's why I've been running the scenarios ahead of time. One of the reasons things didn't go as well as hoped at the last organisation I was at, is that we didn't do anything like enough preparation. So, when staff came to us asking what we planned to do, we had no answers. This time, I plan to make sure that Finance does everything it can do to make sure the executive team can make important decisions in a timely fashion. And, for your information, things started going wrong at my last organisation when the CEO lost his nerve and started lashing out at the people on his team.

Hannah put her head in her hands. 'That was you putting the listening model into action?'

'Yes,' said Michael quietly. 'I made damn sure I understood what she was trying to say. And I listened to her identity, or whatever you call it. I recognised that she's autonomous and pretty directive in her style.'

'I think you had made up your mind already, Michael,' said Hannah quietly. 'Monologue again. You got angry when you heard that these cost reduction scenarios were being discussed outside the Finance team, and you made assumptions about Nicole based on her reaction to the news last week. You may have had the listening model in your mind, but you were absolutely in "defend" mode. You made some pretty big assumptions about Nicole before going to talk to her, without being fully aware as to what was going on for you.'

Michael nodded. 'That's not the worst of it,' he said. 'Turns out that what Tim meant when he said that one or two people in Finance were discussing cost reduction scenarios openly with others in the organisation, was that Nicole herself told Tim and Elaine at lunch.'

'You mean that Nicole had been letting the rest of the executive team know what she was doing?' said Hannah.

'Yes, and she was planning to tell me too.'

'OK,' said Hannah. 'What I'd like you to do is consider the notion of respect. It's hard to really listen to someone, to suspend judgment, to hear everything there is to hear, without coming from a position of respect.'

'Explain to me respect,' said Michael, wondering how he could repair the damage with Nicole.

So, Hannah did.

Respect

First, get out your pencil and fill out the face below (don't worry, you can rub it out later). Draw the face of someone who annoys you, someone whose view you don't want to hear. Draw in their hair too. Or just place the person's photo over the outline.

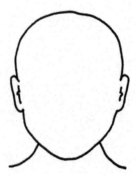

Figure 3

Now find somewhere to sit aside from the busy-ness that surrounds you. Take some deep breaths and relax. Do some mindfulness exercises, if you're into mindfulness. Then ask yourself these questions about the person you have drawn (take your time):

- What do you know about this person?
- What *don't* you know about this person?
- What are you curious about?
- What kind of life have they had?
- How have their experiences and beliefs shaped their values?
- How do their experiences and beliefs show up in their behaviour?
- What do you have in common with this person?

- What annoys you about them?
- What annoys them about you?
- How is this person different to you?
- What are they good at, that you're not good at?
- Is this person a legitimate human being?

See yourself standing facing this person. Notice what is different about you both. Notice what you have in common. See how the 'annoyance' is neither inherent to them nor inherent to you. Seek to respect the person. You can't engage in true dialogue with someone without being able to respect them in the moment.

6 Voicing

In which Michael decides to be brave

After talking to Hannah, Michael realised he had not approached Nicole from a position of genuine respect. He had not suspended various assumptions he held about her, assumptions he hadn't fully been aware of. Now he had some work to do to try and recover the relationship.

He and Hannah had spoken about voicing, another dimension of dialogue. Voicing, she said, was about saying what needed to be said. As she talked, Michael became aware how often he didn't say what needed to be said, for fear of what others might think, or for fear as to how they might react. He was constantly editing what he was saying. Uncomfortable, he recognised how much it mattered what others thought about him, and how this impacted on how open and transparent he was prepared to be.

He thought back to the Town Hall. He had stuck to Elaine's script without deviation. He hadn't allowed himself to share his own thoughts and feelings. He had wanted the rest of the leadership team, especially Elaine, to experience him as the consummate professional. He had wanted the audience to see him as strong and in control. These various 'scripts' about himself, and how he 'should' show up as a leader had got in the way of him sharing aloud his own thoughts. He had stopped short of being open and vulnerable, so making it much less likely that anyone else in the room might speak openly.

Hannah spoke again about respect, and the difference between giving people feedback from a judgmental space and giving people feedback from a respectful space. To receive challenging feedback from someone we don't trust is scary, and our natural response is to defend. To receive challenging feedback from someone who we believe to be on our side is tough too, but often ultimately rewarding.

This time, Michael promised himself, as he walked towards Finance, he would engage in a respectful dialogue with Nicole. He would have another go at the listening thing and focus on his voicing. He acknowledged he was a bit nervous, worried that she might receive his apology as a sign of weakness. But he was confident he was doing this because it felt like the right thing to do. Whether she chose to accept it or not, was up to her. When she saw him approach, Nicole didn't look pleased to see him, but she stood up anyway and went with him to the nearest free meeting room. They both sat down and Michael took a deep breath. He determined to say everything that needed to be said, and to be as authentic as he could.

'I'd like to apologise, Nicole.'

'For what?'

'For not listening to you, and for jumping to conclusions.'

'Go on.'

Michael took another deep breath, before continuing. 'When we interviewed you, you talked about the change programme you led at your previous organisation. I subsequently noticed that their share price plummeted. Instead of asking you about it, I realise now that I just assumed you must have done a poor job.'

Nicole frowned. 'I see.'

'Not on purpose. I didn't even realise. I immediately assumed that because the company share price went down, then the change programme must have been poorly designed. I didn't stop to even realise I was making that assumption. If I had, then hopefully I would have come and asked you about it. When I look at what you've achieved since you've been here …' He stopped himself from talking and decided to listen. 'Well, how do you think things have gone?'

Nicole looked at her hands. 'It's been hard, Michael. I have a good team here in Finance, as you'd know, but it's not easy to get other members of the executive team to engage. That's true for me, and it's true for others in the team, right the way down. I think we all work in siloes, and that makes it hard to get people interested in things they need to get interested in. I'm not looking forward to the next few weeks, to be honest. We will *have* to work together, but I think it's going to be hard.'

Michael nodded. 'I think that's why I recruited you, Nicole. I remember now how hard I found it when I did your role, how dysfunctional the team became. And I think you've done an outstanding job, now I think about it. You've overhauled the whole reporting system and it's all much more accurate and timely.'

'I know other members of the team find me a bit black and white.' Nicole shrugged. 'Perhaps a bit terse on occasion, but I have to speak plainly to be heard. I …' She paused.

'Yes?'

'I'm going to stick my neck out, Michael, and say that you're going to have to lead us differently if we're going to be successful over the next few months.'

Michael breathed deep, feeling for a moment like he was being criticised, tempted to push back in his own defence. But he nodded again instead. 'Tell me more, Nicole, and let's share change stories too.'

7   Reflecting

In which Michael takes time out to think

Michael lay in the bath with a cup of tea at hand. When Hannah had first spoken to him about dialogue, he thought she was talking about a set of skills, a toolbox he could carry around from conversation to conversation. But she told him it was about mindset. He was starting to understand.

It was one thing to tell yourself you were going to listen differently, and to say what needed to be said, but it was hard when you were in the thick of it, being told things you hadn't expected to hear, feeling compelled in the moment to say something, not sure to what extent you were being driven by judgment. He had spoken to Hannah about reflection, and she told him that while it was important to sit and reflect *after* a conversation – and make the time to do that well, it was also important to reflect while *in* the conversation.

He hadn't understood what Hannah meant at the time, but after having spoken to Nicole, now he thought he did. When she told him he needed to lead differently, it felt like a punch to the guts. It took him by surprise. It wasn't fair. Thankfully he had kept quiet and listened to *himself*. He allowed himself to be silent, resisting the temptation to fill the space with words. And in that silence, he recognised that he had already decided he needed to lead differently. Nicole wasn't telling him anything he didn't know already. So why had his first instinct been to push back? Simple. He didn't like the idea that others thought he needed to lead differently. He liked the idea that he was ahead of the game, that he was recognising issues before they became an issue. He liked the idea that he was a great leader. And he was ultimately afraid of the possibility that he was not being a great leader – that he might fail.

Thankfully he had resisted the temptation to respond immediately. He was not the perfect leader, of course he wasn't. And Nicole was offering to give him some feedback that might help him. He needed to respond in a way that would encourage her to continue. He sensed she was nervous, afraid she may have crossed a line. He needed to slow down, to *not* respond. He needed only to ask questions, and listen, to understand.

When he played back the conversation to Hannah, she looked very pleased.

'I think we've done dialogue 101,' she said, smiling. 'Listening, voicing and reflection. Sounds like you've got to grips with engaging in dialogue with people, working one-to-one.'

Michael folded his arms. 'Dialogue 101' made it sound easy. Sounded like there was more to come.

'I'd like to introduce you to Mark,' said Nicole. 'He can help you introduce dialogue to the team.'

'The team?'

'The team.' She nodded. 'Whichever way you look at it, your team sits at the heart of the change you want to happen.'

'Tim, Nicole, Elaine, Con, Karen, and Jo,' said Michael thoughtfully, 'the Magnificent Seven.'

'Not so magnificent in the eyes of many employees,' said Hannah. 'You need to change that.'

Part II
Michael and Mark

8 Mark

In which Mark meets Michael

Mark stood on the opposite side of the road gazing at the six-storey office. If Hannah was to be believed, he would be coming here often. Successful team coaching assignments often lasted 12 months or more, during which time he got to know the people on those teams like he knew some of his closest friends. Every assignment was different, every assignment was challenging, every assignment was exhausting at times, and every assignment was ultimately rewarding. He wondered what this one would be like, and what he would learn?

Last time he spoke to Hannah she had been thinking of leaving. Working for a Head of HR who didn't seem to really get 'change', at least in the way that Hannah thought of it. Now she was working directly with the CEO. He still didn't understand how that happened, but Hannah seemed energised and excited. She said she was confident this guy, Michael, was committed to the long haul. He hoped it really was the case. He'd seen so many senior leaders bale out at critical moments of the change process, when the going got tough.

Crossing the road, he noticed the café on the ground floor of the building. It was lunchtime, yet the café was barely half full. Just a long line of people waiting for take-aways. What did that say about this organisation? He got into the elevator with three other people. Two of them gazed at their phones, listening to something through headpieces. The other one just gazed at the lift door as if in a trance. No one made eye contact. Mark stepped out onto the sixth floor and headed to the reception desk. A man and a woman sat talking to each other. It took him a few seconds to attract their attention. Then one of them asked him to wait.

'Hi Mark,' said Hannah, stepping out from behind a glass door. 'Great to see you! Let me introduce you to Michael.'

Michael was well dressed, thought Mark, trim, mid-forties. More grey hairs than you might expect, looking a bit tired. They sat around a low rectangular coffee table and Hannah started the conversation. Mark and Michael shared stories about what they'd done in the past by way of introduction, and Michael outlined what was going on, outside and inside the organisation, and voiced some of his hopes and fears for the next few months/years.

'So,' Michael concluded. 'Hannah said you'd be the best person to work with us as a team.'

'Happy to consider it,' Mark agreed. 'Let me start by asking, what's your purpose for this piece of work?'

'I need the team to work better together,' Michael replied. 'Simple as that.'

'In service of what?' said Mark, thinking life is never simple.

'Leading this organisation effectively through the next two years,' said Michael. 'We have all sorts of challenges coming our way and we need to manage them together. At the moment, everyone looks after their own patch. We made an acquisition a couple of years ago, which didn't go well. People still identify with the old companies and not the new. Morale is low and we've lost key people. The recent government announcement has people wondering if they still have a job. I'm worried more key staff will leave over the coming weeks.'

'Hmm,' Mark replied. 'What's going well?'

Michael raised a brow. 'Good question. I haven't been thinking about the good stuff much recently. Let's see. He lifted a finger. First, we have some good people, including the folks on the leadership team. They don't work together very effectively, but with one exception I think they're the people we need to take the business forward. Two, we have good products. We may lose a quarter of our business, but the other 75 per cent is in pretty good shape. Three, we have time to put this right – we just need to use the time wisely. Four, we have you to help us out.'

Mark smiled. 'Thanks for the vote of confidence. Now tell me again what the purpose of the team piece is, and what success looks like.'

'I would like to see the team working together on the things they need to be working on together if we are to be successful as a business,' Mark replied. 'And I would like the rest of the business to be saying they have confidence in our capacity to lead.'

'Great,' said Mark. 'Now I'm beginning to understand your perspective. I need to talk to everyone else on the team as well. But first let's talk about what might lie ahead.'

Then he took Mark through the Beanacre Model.

The Beanacre Model

Mark took Michael through the Beanacre Model only to the extent required for Michael to get a sense of what was to happen. He didn't get the sense Michael was interested in hearing a lot of theory, and the best way of coming to understand the model anyway, was to experience it.

The Beanacre Model was Mark's guide to taking a team to a place where dialogue was most likely to happen. It started with *contracting*, a process through which Mark, Michael, and the rest of the team would agree on the purpose for dialogue. This wasn't a one-off process. The business was embarking on a long and complex journey. They would need to contract and re-contract as they went.

Mark, in his role, would need to talk to team members, *preparing* them for what was to come, and preparing himself besides. He would need to check out the location, do some *scene setting*, in creating a physical environment most conducive to dialogue.

At the heart of the process sits the *container*. Mark didn't spend too much time at this point explaining the nature of the container to

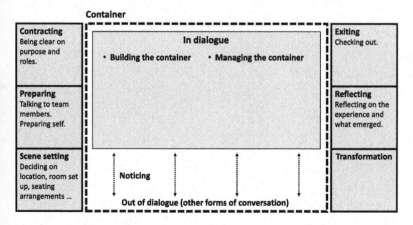

Figure 4 Beanacre Model

Michael. Suffice to say at this stage, that one of his roles as process facilitator, was to facilitate the emergence of a safe space in which people were most likely to suspend judgment and say what needed to be said. At various times, there would be an *exiting* process, as people walked away from the container, followed by some time spent *reflecting*.

Transformation was more an outcome of the whole group dialogic process.

As predicted, Michael didn't fully understand what Mark was saying, but declared himself ready to begin the journey! Mark was happy though. He knew Michael's understanding of the model would develop through their experience of working together.

9 Talking to the team

In which Mark reflects on meeting with team members

Mark sat on a bench in a nearby park, paper and pens on his lap. As he reflected on what he heard, he drew a diagram, with everyone's name on it.

He thought about the team mandate. People all had different agendas. Michael saw his mandate as being to steady the company, negating the threat of losing a quarter of their business. Tim talked about David, a board member, who wanted the team to develop new markets in Eastern Europe and South-East Asia. Nicole was focused on the numbers, making sure no one did the wrong thing, and trying to influence the Board to put in place a more robust governance process. Elaine was focused on lobbying the Government on the new proposals and Con spoke only of growing year-on-year sales, no matter what. Karen didn't seem to have much of an agenda. It took ages to track her down and then she cut their conversation short.

Although there were a multitude of agendas at play, and no clear team goals nor strategy, these agendas didn't appear contradictory. There was a common agenda in there somewhere, Mark thought. He knew he would need to interview the Board members as well, to find out what their expectations were, and a few key clients.

The team dynamics were interesting. Michael was relying heavily on Tim, Nicole and Elaine to get things done. They operated as a team within a team, with the four of them making most of the decisions, much to the annoyance of Con. Karen appeared to be completely sidelined and disengaged, while Jo seemed happy on the sidelines. She sat on the Board along with Michael and identified most with that role. Con didn't seem to get along with anyone, and so Mark drew a big red circle around his name. Con was the only person on the leadership team from the company that had been acquired. Tim and Nicole were new, while the rest were heritage. Tim, Con and Karen gave conflicting accounts of each other's responsibilities and were confused as to who was supposed to be doing what.

They showed few signs of working as a team, with most people communicating through Michael, such that Michael was operating like the hub of a bicycle wheel. No wonder he looked tired, Mark thought. Bottom line was that none of them thought they worked particularly well together and none of them knew what to do about it. Karen didn't seem to care and Con hinted at leaving.

It was interesting too to hear how they each described the company. Michael talked about the organisation as if it were a battlefield, wounded soldiers lying about the place, recovering from the acquisition 'battle', too exhausted to face what lies ahead in the coming months. Nicole talked about the organisation as if it was a hospital too, but in a different sense. She talked about the doctors, the nurses, the different departments, all working independently of each other to get things done, including her own function. She saw it as her role to hold things together, by making sure the numbers are right, and putting in good process to make sure nothing falls through the cracks. Tim compared the organisation to a government department, obsessed by process and incapable of innovation. It seemed likely he and Nicole would clash at some point, if they hadn't already. They could do with a new metaphor, Mark thought.

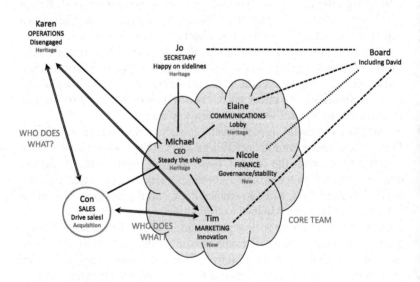

Figure 5 A system

As he drew the system as he saw it, he began to understand at least some of what was happening, to notice where dialogue was happening in the system and where it probably wasn't.

'Big job ahead,' he muttered to himself, surprising a boy riding past on his bicycle.

10 Mark's 'plan'

In which Mark tells Michael what to expect

Michael, Mark and Hannah sat in Michael's office. Mark had just finished debriefing Michael as to what he had learned, carefully restricting his commentary to some of the broader patterns he had noticed, without disclosing who said what.

'So, tell me, Mark. What's the plan?' said Michael. 'And help me understand how it fits with your Beanie model.'

'Beanacre,' said Mark. 'And if you remember, the next stage is to meet up. Container building is next on the agenda.'

'Container building,' said Michael. 'Sounds like the sort of thing a therapist would say.'

Mark nodded. 'I guess, but I'm not sure how else to put it. And I think it's a pretty good metaphor. Let me explain.'

Michael nodded. 'Try.'

'Hannah tells me that you and she have been having conversations about dialogue, in terms of listening, voicing and reflection, in terms of suspending and defending, in terms of respecting others. Is that right?'

'Yes,' said Michael. 'And she's talked about the dialogic mindset, which is more jargon as far as I'm concerned.'

He's in a bad mood, thought Mark. 'Hannah told me about your Town Hall too.'

'She talks about that a lot,' said Michael.

'What happened at your Town Hall is a wonderful example of what happens when the container is absent,' Mark explained. 'It's not a safe place for people to speak up and say what needs to be said. It's not a place conducive to great listening. People tend to lock into their own thought processes. There isn't the space for people to put aside their suspicions and concerns to be able to truly suspend whatever's going on for them, to hear others from a position of respect. As a result – no dialogue.'

'Hannah explained that,' said Michael.

'Creating a container for a hundred people to feel safe to engage in dialogue is not impossible, but it is hard to achieve,' said Mark. 'Getting back to the team work, my role is to facilitate the creation of a container in which the seven of you feel safe engaging in dialogue with each other. I can't make you be in dialogue, but I can facilitate the conditions under which it is most likely to happen.'

Michael nodded.

Mark continued. 'Once the container is formed then we will need to heat things up a bit. You may hear me talk about disturbance or perturbance. That's about stirring things up so that behavioural patterns can emerge, patterns I can help you pay attention to and work with.'

'Right,' said Michael. 'So, you apply heat to the container so we can see for ourselves how we're operating as a team.'

'Right,' said Mark. 'But we don't turn the heat up too high, because we want to stay in relationship, and the patterns we're looking for are conversational patterns. By noticing the patterns, you can change the ones that aren't serving you well and emerge from the container working differently together. That's the work of a dialogic team coach.'

'Like a butterfly emerging from a cocoon,' said Michael.

'Quite,' said Hannah.

'Better fix a date then,' said Michael.

11 Mark prepares himself

In which Mark prepares to work with Michael's team

The first session with Michael's team was tomorrow. Mark always made sure he allowed himself a few hours the day before a first session to prepare himself. Some practitioners see themselves as externals or visitors, outside the dynamics of the team. If challenged, they turn the attention of the team back onto their own dynamics. These folks often set rules for their sessions, which include being polite to the facilitator. If challenged, to the extent it becomes uncomfortable, they remind the team of the rules. If that doesn't work then, regrettably, they often leave the team to manage for themselves.

The dialogic approach is different. When a group of people gather in a room, everyone is engaged in the dialogic process, like it or not. Every utterance has an impact on the flow of conversation and is data for the facilitator about what's going on in the system. Mark saw his role as guide and explorer. It was his job to pay attention to the container, to notice the extent to which the container was present or not. He couldn't *make* a team engage in dialogue, but he could facilitate the conditions for dialogue to take place. This wasn't always easy. Not everyone wants to engage in dialogue. There are always one or two people, at least, who resist. This resistance is often channelled directly at the facilitator. Or at someone else in the team, in which case it would be Mark's job to help the team understand what was going on, and why, without judgment or blame.

He would be tested. You never knew in advance what would happen, he thought to himself, and it was important not to make assumptions, but you could hypothesise. For example, in this case he sensed underlying tensions between Tim and Nicole. Those tensions would likely be directed at him. At some point Karen's behaviour would get called out. Con's anger about the way the acquisition was managed would surface, and likely be directed at Michael. These were just some of the dynamics happening in the team of which he was already aware. There was a lot else going on too, dynamics he hadn't yet come across. Sometimes it was tempting to let tensions roll by, let themselves crash upon the beach like waves and disperse. But every time he let something pass, without commenting upon it, he would be establishing a norm. Every time he *did* call something out, he would also be establishing a norm.

The boundaries of the container they co-created would to a great extent be determined by the way in which he personally role modelled dialogue. If he chose not to call something out, others would know. They would, consciously or otherwise, be led by him in deciding how safe it was to speak their minds. They would notice the extent to which he was able to hear what others said without becoming defensive, reverting to monologue, and behaving accordingly.

Mark lay back on the sofa and reflected once more on some of his triggers. He had felt triggered by Michael already. The way he talked about 'jargon' and declared himself to be somewhat ignorant of the process. He had felt Michael 'abandoning' him, feelings that evoked old memories of finding himself unexpectedly alone. If Michael was showing up like this in the meeting with Hannah, then he was pretty sure the same behaviour would show up in the team meeting. He would need to manage his instinctive reaction, which was to withdraw within himself. He would need to call out Michael's behaviour, enquiring about it without prejudice or predetermination. Then there was Karen. This process would be hard for her. At some point, someone was likely to draw attention to the way she chose not to engage with the rest of the team. When that happened, others would likely join in. If Mark wasn't careful he would find himself slipping into rescue mode, withholding his own observations as to the way Karen behaved, and finding his ability to listen compromised by a desire to keep her safe.

Big day ahead, thought Mark to himself. 'Facilitator – know thyself,' he said quietly, before closing his eyes and connecting more deeply with his thoughts and feelings.

12 Setting the scene

In which Mark sets up a circle

Mark persuaded Michael to schedule the first team session alongside a team offsite, already planned. He arrived at the conference centre two hours before the session was due to start and met with Hannah. A staff member led them to a large boardroom with no windows. The staff member's name was Robert and he said he was in charge of events.

'This isn't what we asked for, Robert,' said Hannah calmly.

Mark stared at the huge boardroom table that took up the whole of the middle of the room. He crouched down to look underneath and saw it was fixed permanently in position. The last thing he wanted was to have the team all sat in a rectangle with a great sea of wood and steel forming a barrier between them. He already had visions of the seven of them playing with their phones under the table while he facilitated introductions.

'This is the room you used last time,' said Robert.

Hannah nodded. 'I wasn't here last time, so I'll take your word for it. But if you look at the request form you'll see we asked for a good-sized room with natural light and no big tables, just a simple circle of chairs. This room may have been appropriate for the team's needs last time, but we can't use it for this meeting.'

Robert looked distraught. 'I thought it was a senior executive team meeting?'

'It is,' Hannah smiled.

'And they want to sit in a *circle*?' Robert asked. 'All the executive teams we work with like the boardroom.'

'What does the circle mean to you?' asked Mark, from beneath the boardroom table.

'Well,' stammered Robert. 'Isn't that like what they do in therapy?'

'I think so,' said Mark, getting to his feet. 'I don't know, I'm not a therapist. The point of the circle is quite simple. The circle, just a ring of chairs, is the best set up in terms of people being able to see each other.'

He pointed to the boardroom table. 'If I'm sitting towards the top of the table on this side, it's actually quite difficult to see the person sitting down the other end of the table on the opposite side. And all this wood …' He waved a hand. 'Great for spreading out your papers, but it means I can't see your hands, can't see your feet. I can *hear* what everyone else is saying, but I can't *see* what they're saying.'

'Nothing wrong with your table,' said Hannah, touching Robert's arm. 'I think the team are planning to use it tomorrow, but not today.'

'I see,' said Robert. 'Let me show you what else we have.'

Circles and setting

People in organisations don't often sit in circles. They spend more time sitting about tables, round or rectangular. The circle can be confronting. Any anxieties people feel about sitting in a circle make it likely that the facilitator will be challenged. Those anxieties may show up as comments such as '*I didn't know we were going to do therapy*', or people bursting into versions of '*Kumbaya, my Lord*'.

The reason many dialogic facilitators encourage people to sit in a circle is simply that it offers best line of sight. Every person can see clearly every other person. This makes it easier for people to pay attention to what others are saying, to notice body language, and to be heard. The circle is also indifferent to hierarchy. There is no special chair for the leader or facilitator. This makes it more likely that all voices will be heard and respected. In short, the circle makes dialogue easier and helps with container building.

Of course, sitting in a circle doesn't by itself mean you will get dialogue. Sitting in a circle isn't the same as engaging in dialogue. By the same token, if you choose not to sit in a circle, it doesn't mean you won't succeed in stimulating dialogue.

Seating arrangements are not the only factor to consider. What other decisions can you make to make it easier for people to focus on each other, undistracted? You might choose somewhere away from the office perhaps, away from other staff who can interrupt in the event of a 'crisis'. Away from the temptation of stepping out for five minutes to make sure that important thing gets done. Somewhere quiet. Somewhere that encourages reflection, listening and courageous speech.

On the other hand, perhaps you don't want to take people away to a quiet place. Perhaps you want to 'bring the system into the room' so that you can work directly with the impact of that system. You might choose to work with an executive team in a meeting room in the middle of one of their call centres, for example, or with a health board in a

Figure 6

training room at the heart of a hospital. Why would you take the team somewhere so potentially distracting? So they can see for themselves the impact of the system on their way of operating. The choices you make will be determined by the needs of the team and their purpose for wanting to work with you.

13 Check-in

In which team members have the opportunity to share what's really on their minds

First session. Some of the team arrived early, some on time, and a couple of people were ten minutes late, including Michael. Mark noticed a couple of thoughts pop up in his head. Hadn't they agreed yesterday that Michael would arrive half an hour before the meeting was due to start? Was Michael truly committed to this process? Had Hannah truly succeeded in gaining Michael's commitment to the team coaching?

'Sorry,' said Michael to everyone as he arrived, and then to Mark especially. 'Rebecca had an accident last night. Fell off her bike at the skate-park. Wasn't supposed to be at the skate-park and wasn't supposed to be on her brother's bike. Broke her arm in three places. Heather's been at the hospital with her all night and I had to take Luke to school. I should have called and let everyone know what was going on.' He looked around the room, noticed the ring of chairs, and wondered what to do with his bag and coat.

'Take your time,' said Mark. 'Your head must still be spinning. Why don't you put your bag and coat over there, grab a coffee and then we can begin.'

'Before I ask Michael to kick us off with some context,' said Mark. 'I'd like to do a check-in.' A few people nodded as if they knew what he meant. 'The purpose of a check-in,' said Mark, 'is to put out there anything on people's minds, anything it may be useful for others to know. It can be anything, anything at all, anything that might get in the way of you being fully present today. There are just two rules for checking in. First, everyone says something. Second, no one responds to what others say or interrupts. Everyone can speak for as long or as little as they like too. We have time, there's no rush.'

'What if I'm curious?' asked Michael.

'You can ask questions later.' said Mark. 'The purpose of the check-in is to help the team as a whole, understand where individuals are at, and to help people be present with each other.'

'OK,' said Michael. 'I'll start then.' He put his hands on his knees and puffed out his cheeks. 'My heart is still pounding. Rebecca broke her arm badly last night and was in dreadful pain. They'll probably need to operate. We won't know until lunchtime. To be honest that's all I've been thinking about the last 12 hours. I wasn't sure whether to go ahead with today's session or not. Part of me thinks I should really be at the hospital with Heather, but I decided we need to do this. I'll call Heather at morning tea time and see how things are going. There is a possibility I'll need to leave early.'

Michael looked to Mark, and Mark again noticed thoughts popping up in his head, as he anticipated what he might do were the meeting to be truncated. He said nothing to Michael though, and looked to see who else might speak. It wouldn't be Karen, he guessed. She sat, slightly slumped in her chair, looking thoroughly bored.

'I'll go next,' said Nicole. 'I understand that today is about discussing how we can work better as a team. I'm glad we're here. I'm sorry to hear about Rebecca, Michael, and if you need to go, then I think you should go. If this session is going to be of any value, then we need you to be here 100 per cent.' She paused and took a deep breath. 'I am feeling quite stressed actually. As some of you know, we've been running some scenarios on costs, so that we're ready to support the tough discussions. Whichever way you look at it, we have some big decisions to make. No one has said anything, but some of the people doing the analysis are already worrying what the consequences will be for them. I do think we need to spend this time together, but part of me says I should be with my team right now.'

There was a silence after Nicole finished.

'I'll go next,' said Mark, to some people's surprise. 'I've spoken to all of you individually in preparing for today and, as always before a session, I've found myself playing through various scenarios as to how things might play out. I don't want to be distracted by those scenarios or make assumptions about what will happen. Also, I got a wee bit stressed out this morning when we arrived and found we'd been put in the wrong room, and again when Michael didn't arrive at the time we agreed. So, I'm still just tuning in.'

Karen snorted and prepared to speak, arms still folded. 'I'm not sure why we're here,' she said. 'I've got a lot on my plate, which I need to get done. I've had it explained to me, but I don't agree with it.'

There was a longer pause this time. Most people looked at Michael, to see how he'd react, but he just nodded, calm.

'I think it's good we're here,' said Tim. 'Though I would like to have received an agenda. I'd like to make sure we have time to talk about strategy. It might help Nicole's team feel better if we started talking about some growth options, not just cost reduction. Other than that, I'm fine.'

'I agree with Tim, to some extent anyway,' said Elaine. 'My team will focus all our energies on the lobbying process, but we should assume there will be significant changes. I'm glad Nicole's team are thinking ahead, because if we are going to be making redundancies, we need to be ready to make decisions and expedite the process quickly. We can't allow the process to drag out, otherwise the whole company will just end up in gridlock. I'm worried that rumours start circulating, people get anxious, the unions get involved, and that by the time we recover we find ourselves in a desperate position. We're going to need to be decisive and make sure we control the message.'

She looked at Michael, who again stayed quiet.

'This whole company is just one big rumour mill,' said Con. 'You can't control the message. Too many people felt they got shafted by the acquisition, last year. The company said one thing and did another. We must be much more open and transparent. I'll be very interested to see what happens today.' He looked at Mark. 'To see just how open and transparent we're prepared to be with each other. I have my doubts.'

'Interesting,' said Jo, speaking last. 'I sense we're already surfacing some of the tensions in this team. The recent announcements have just made things harder. I do think you need to think about how you will work together more effectively moving forward.'

Mark thanked everyone. He had planned to next invite Michael to speak, but he noticed himself reflecting on what he'd just heard. If others were thinking the same, then he doubted anyone else would be listening deeply to Michael set context. So instead he invited the team to reflect together on what they'd heard. They talked for two hours until someone called for a toilet break.

When Mark reflected at lunch on how the session went, he realised how concerned he had been as to how Michael would show up. Would he assume a leadership role, or would he drift to the sidelines? In that context, his daughter's accident seemed almost incredible, the perfect excuse to arrive late and declare himself distracted. And yet he hadn't cancelled the meeting. What was happening there? Nicole was the first to explicitly name the worries people felt about the proposed new laws – interestingly Michael hadn't. But everyone else took Nicole's lead, using the check-in process to declare their views as to what needed to happen next. Except for Karen. Karen seemed to have checked out already from the team. She openly opposed the process and said little in the conversation that followed, though she stayed in the session until the end. Jo also seemed checked out, but in a different sense. She spoke as if she wasn't a member of the team herself, but as if she was a concerned onlooker.

'The power of the check-in,' said Mark to himself, before making himself a cup of tea.

Checking in and checking out

To engage in dialogue is to be as present as one can be, whether that's one-on-one or in a group. It's hard to be present if we are distracted, and so one role of the facilitator is to create an environment that offers the opportunity for people to be more fully present in the moment. Regardless of the setting, people often turn up to conversations distracted by things happening somewhere else. Especially these days, when most people are very busy, and we have various devices that allow us to be in contact 24 hours a day, every day, with people all over the world.

To put it another way, we arrive at dialogue with 'baggage', the baggage of what else is happening in our worlds, what's likely to distract us. Unless we each open our baggage and show others what's in the case, they don't know, and if they don't know – they make assumptions. Like – he's bored, she's not interested in what I have to say etc. The *check-in* is a device that helps people tune into each other and to begin listening differently. Even telling others what else is going on in our lives helps us recognise our own distractions, helping us prepare more effectively to engage in dialogue.

Another function of the check-in, when working with groups and teams, is that it gets everyone's voice into the room right at the beginning. Everyone is heard, knowing that they won't be challenged or have their point of view dismissed. The check-in is an opportunity for people to start practising listening, suspending and respecting. This is why it's useful to establish a rule that says, 'no interruption, no response.' The interruption or response is usually monologic, at a time when the team is trying to get into dialogue.

The *check-out* plays a similar function in reverse. When we exit dialogue, and walk away from the conversation, we walk away with our interpretation of that experience. If we don't check out with each other, we will likely make assumptions about others experience of the conversation, only to find out later we've all walked away having made different assumptions. This may create problems, sometimes big problems. The check-out is an opportunity for people to share what they're putting back into their suitcase as they prepare to leave, to share what feelings and thoughts they are having, and any actions they have committed to as a consequence of what emerged from the dialogue.

14 Container building

In which the team dare to dream

After lunch Mark spoke about the principles of dialogue. He didn't spend a lot of time on the subject, just enough that they could begin to share a common language through which they could reflect upon the way they related to each other. He talked about listening, and the value of being able to suspend judgment, in service of understanding the other. He talked about voicing, and the need to bring challenge into the room. A couple of people said they felt inhibited by the circle, that it reminded them of previous experiences in which they had felt obliged to give each other positive feedback and *suppress* challenge. Mark acknowledged some of the difficulties in challenging others openly in front of the rest of the team. As they talked, Mark noticed Tim go quiet. He looked agitated.

'What's happening, Tim?' he asked.

'I'd really like it if we stopped talking theory and got into the real discussion,' said Tim. 'We need to talk strategy. What are we going to do?'

'In service of going where?' asked Mark.

'In service of moving this business forward,' said Tim. 'We can't spend all day talking about how best to get along with each other. We must come up with a plan. We all know these laws will come into effect in some form or another. We can't just wait.'

'Right,' said Mark. He considered what to say next. Co-creating a purpose for dialogue was all part of building the container, but Tim seemed to be voicing a blanket reluctance to talking about team dynamics, a reluctance that would have to be called out sooner or later. Now might not be the right time, he thought. 'Do you think you're all agreed as to what the future of the business looks like?' Mark asked the team.

'Undoubtedly not,' said Jo. 'Tim wants to go off and invest in new markets, while Michael and Nicole want to take their time. Elaine wants to control the message, and Con wants an organisation in which everyone is open and transparent.'

'Those are some of the differences,' said Mark. 'Are there any commonalities in terms of what you'd all like for this company?'

'We all want growth,' said Con. 'And we all want this to be a great place to work. We may have different ideas as to what that looks like, but surely we're all agreed on that?'

Everyone nodded, except Karen.

'Great,' said Mark. 'Then let's talk about that. How about each of you in turn talks about what it would be like to wake up in the morning, a year from now, when the company is growing and everyone's enjoying themselves. How about we each take just a few minutes to think about that, before sharing our ideas with the rest of the team? During the sharing process, I'll invite you, to begin with, just to listen.'

'Listening for intention and identity,' said Michael, sticking one finger in the air. 'I remember that from class.'

Mark became aware again how easy it was for him to feel triggered by Michael. He let the feeling pass before inviting Michael to share what he meant. Michael seized upon the invitation and explained the Listening Model with real energy and enthusiasm. Instead of sounding sceptical, he sought permission from Nicole to recount their difficult conversation. Nicole agreed, nodding slowly and Michael shared the story. By the time he finished everyone in the room was still. Something had shifted. The container, thought Mark to himself, watching Michael. He's just helped us all take an important step forward.

The team spent the next two hours sharing perspectives as to what the company might look like. Mark intervened occasionally, both noticing when challenge was absent from the conversation, and at the same time daring people to think big. Everyone seemed engaged, including Tim. But not Karen.

Building the container

Lots of people talk about container building. Isaacs suggests there are five dimensions the facilitator may leverage to create the right conditions for dialogue (see Table 2).

Reflecting on the choice he made in building on Tim's suggestion to focus on purpose, Mark recognised he had leaned into an opportunity

Table 2

Evoke the ideal	Dialogue is purposeful. That doesn't mean the group must enter dialogue with specific goals and KPIs. It means that there is a sense that something new and impactful will emerge from the conversation. Supporting the articulation of this potential can help create the container.
Support dreaming out loud	In most of the conversations we have, we make judgments as to what to share and what not to share. We may worry about what others think. We anticipate judgment and frame our contributions accordingly. To access unguarded, unadulterated contributions from others requires creating the space where people feel supported and respected.
Deepen the listening	Dialogue requires listening curiously, without judgment. The facilitator can invite the group to notice from time to time, how people are listening.
Make it safe for opposers	Listening is not the same as agreeing. If people equate the two, then people will edit their voicing, and dialogue won't happen. It must be legitimate to challenge, respectfully. Again, the facilitator has an important role to play.
Dare people to suspend	How do people respond to the challenge? Do they defend what they said, or open themselves up to the possibility of other perspectives?

to 'evoke the ideal', and to encourage team members to 'dream out loud'. He would have to call out Tim's opposition to spending time working on interpersonal relationships at some point, if no one else did, but it had felt too early. Tim's challenge had been respectful, and at this early stage of the process it was great for the team to experience an effective challenge. Mark wondered how quickly others would follow.

15 Revolt

In which Karen gets triangulated

Mark met with the team again two weeks later. After the team checked in, the conversation turned to how the team operated together. Con and Tim got into an argument.

'The problem with you, Con,' said Tim, 'is that you think short term all the time. Quarterly sales targets, monthly sales targets, how much we've sold in an afternoon. You don't think strategically.'

'Strategy is a word used by people who don't know how to generate sales,' replied Con, with a sneer. 'We've had strategists here before you came along. They spent two years strategizing, then buggered off having delivered nothing.'

'What's happening now?' Mark asked the group, trying to intervene.

Tim ignored him. 'Mate, left up to you we'll still be trying to sell the same products to the same people in ten years' time. You'll be the bloke on the corner trying to flog Kodak Instamatics.'

'Let me ask again,' Mark said. 'What's happening now?'

'They're debating,' said Jo. 'Neither is seeking to understand the other. They're doing monologue.'

Mark waited for someone else to speak.

'It's unlikely anything useful will emerge from the conversation,' said Nicole. 'Everyone else has gone quiet. I know I'm reluctant to say anything, for fear of being beaten down.'

There was a long pause.

'So tell me, mate,' said Tim through clenched teeth. 'Tell me more about "strategy".'

Con shrugged and muttered something before looking to his hands. The group sat quiet again for a couple of minutes, then Michael intervened.

'Let's start again,' he said. 'How do we currently work together? We've all heard Mark report back his perspective as to how we operate. What do others think?'

'The bit about the core team was right,' said Karen, surprising everyone. 'There are four people in this team. The rest of us are hangers-on.' She sat back on her chair, looked to the ceiling and crossed her hands.

'That's bullshit!' said Tim, loudly. 'There are seven in this team, but not everyone shows up. You're the worst. You don't come to team meetings. You're never available to talk to. It's like you've given up. I don't know what's going through your head, but to me you're a dead weight.'

Karen didn't move, but Mark saw her eyes fill with tears, before she snapped to her feet and left the room. Michael got up and followed.

'Well played, Tim,' said Nicole, shaking her head. 'Way to go.'

Mark left the room to find out what was happening. He saw Michael stood at the end of the corridor, close to Karen, who was looking to the floor. They appeared deep in conversation, with Michael doing most of the talking. After a few minutes, they both walked slowly back towards him. They re-entered the room, Karen still head down. The team sat quiet again, waiting for Mark to say something.

'I'd like to offer you another lens on what just happened,' he said. 'but before I do that, Tim, do you want to share what was going on for you?'

'Yes. I lost it.' He looked to Karen. 'Apologies, Karen. No excuses. Not sure what came over me, but that was very unprofessional. There are ways to say things, and that wasn't the right way. Monologue or dialogue, I don't know, but that was completely disrespectful. I'm sorry.'

'Monologue, I think,' muttered Nicole.

Mark then explained triangulation, deliberately steering the conversation away from content, and towards process.

Triangulation

There are numerous models for thinking about what happens between people in a team or group. Mark found himself noticing with reference to *triangulation*. This idea of triangulation is one of several aspects of family systems described by Murray Bowen. According to Bowen every one-to-one relationship is unstable to some extent, even the very best and strongest relationships. There is always some anxiety in a relationship at some point in time. That anxiety tends to be discharged onto a third person, and the triangle is the smallest stable relationship.

In this case the relationship is the relationship between Con, Tim and Karen. Mark is already aware that there exists tension in this relationship; he has already learned that the three of them find it hard to agree who's responsible for what. All three of them have already told him stories of two or all of them arguing.

In this meeting, Con and Tim have already had an argument. Although the argument stopped, it was evident to everyone that Con

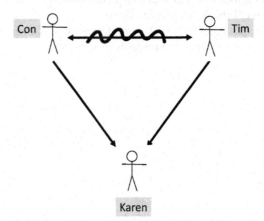

Figure 7 Triangulation

and Tim were still angry with each other. Think of their relationship like an electric storm, just waiting for a lightning rod to appear, through which that tension could be discharged. Karen was always the most likely candidate to play that role, and sure enough she spoke up, even though she had said little in any of their sessions so far.

Mark knows all about triangulation, because it's often the facilitator who gets triangulated on when there is tension in the room, particularly when a team is just getting going. Until the container is built, there is always unexpressed tension in the system, and it has to be discharged somewhere! If Mark is to manage tensions inside the container, he may need to call attention to these patterns, and help people to understand what is going on. He will need to help people to step aside from the *content* of the conversations in which they are participating, to focus on those conversations as a *process*.

16 Perturbance

In which Mark turns up the heat

When Mark arrived at the next session, the team looked happy. Tim and Nicole chatted and laughed with each other. Elaine, Con and Michael stood together drinking coffee. Jo sat on her own scrolling e-mails. At the check-in, they all talked about how much more comfortable they felt with each other, except for Jo, who talked about how everyone *else* in the team seemed to feel more comfortable with each other and how good that was to see. Once they'd finished checking-in the group waited for Mark to say something.

Mark noticed how polite everyone was being with each other. 'What isn't being said here?' he asked himself. Time to introduce a little perturbance.

'I'm noticing,' he said, 'that Karen isn't here, and yet no one has called out her absence.' A few people looked to the floor. Others looked at Michael. Con frowned.

No one said anything for two minutes. Mark became aware of the container, and wondered how strong it was, and to what extent the team would succeed in surfacing whatever it was that bubbled away beneath the surface.

'Well, I don't think it was done well,' said Con, at last, staring at his hands. 'I only found out by e-mail that she was leaving. I think we should have talked about it. When people asked me why she was leaving, I didn't feel able to respond as I would have liked.'

'I agree,' said Elaine quietly, looking at Michael. 'We have to get better at communicating the message.'

'I know that there are aspects of Karen's departure that must remain confidential,' said Nicole, 'but I would like to know more about what happened, and what processes were followed. Not least because I wouldn't like the same to happen to me.'

There was silence again.

'Well I guess you're all waiting for me to say something,' said Michael. 'Con and Elaine, I take your points on board, I could and should have communicated it better. But it had to be done, and I imagine you all know why.'

'I don't know why,' said Con. 'I can guess, but I don't know.' Tim and Nicole both nodded in agreement.

'Very well,' said Michael. 'I had concerns about the performance of Operations, in particular the way that other departments seemed to feel it was difficult to work with that function. I flagged those concerns to Karen on several occasions, but she didn't agree with me. I listened to what she had to say. Indeed, I put a lot of effort into listening.' He looked at Mark. 'But it seemed very clear to me that we weren't on the same page, so I invited her to seek opportunities elsewhere. The company is doing all it can to support her in finding another role, in an organisation more suited to her talents and capabilities.'

There was silence once more.

'What did you all hear?' asked Mark.

Con shook his head. 'Not much,' he said. 'Sounded like a press release.'

'Right,' said Mark, acknowledging Con's courage in speaking up. 'Can I ask you Michael, what it feels like to hear Con say that?'

Michael cleared his throat and looked to the ceiling. 'It feels hard,' he said. 'I feel squeezed between wanting to tell you all everything that took place, and respecting Karen's position in all of this. I'm not sure what I should share and what I shouldn't.'

'And you chose not to tell us very much,' said Jo. 'So, I'm wondering what that says about how much you trust this team.'

'I don't think this is the forum,' said Elaine, cheeks flushed. 'Michael has said all he can say, in my view. Karen wasn't performing to expectations, so he asked her to leave. That's all we need to know.'

'Well, it leaves me feeling unclear,' said Tim.

'Me too,' said Nicole.

'OK,' said Michael, drawing a breath. 'Then let me explain. I didn't ask Karen to leave because Operations wasn't meeting the plan. I asked her to leave because she wouldn't engage in conversation as to what the causes of that poor performance might be. Every time I asked her what the issue was, she pointed the finger at other functions and blamed them for making her life difficult. I couldn't get her to identify one thing that Operations might do differently, that she felt they could take responsibility for. Not only did I find it hard to engage with her personally, but she didn't appear to be working well with any of you. Several of you have commented in the past how hard you've found it to engage with her. I made the time to watch her and saw her decline the opportunity to work with her peers. I asked her time and time again to explain to me her perspective on things, but I didn't get anywhere. If we as a company are going to succeed, then we have to collaborate and Karen didn't collaborate.'

'So, it's our fault?' said Tim. 'You did it because you thought we wanted you to.'

Michael shook his head. 'I looked at what I thought was going on, and I made a decision, based on what I felt needed to happen for the sake of the business.'

There was a short silence, followed by further discussion. Mark then switched the focus of the conversation.

'How did you experience the last 40 minutes?' he asked. 'What happened?'

'It didn't feel like dialogue at the beginning,' said Nicole. 'I think we had all been thinking about Karen's leaving, but chose not to talk about it. That says we still have more work to do in building trust. And when we did start talking about it, it became clear that some of us were angry with Michael for not telling us what was going on. That anger was getting in the way of our listening.'

'I felt like I was being circled upon,' said Michael. 'It felt like sitting in the lion's cage. Then you all stopped growling and started to ask me questions. At the beginning, it felt like you'd all made your minds up and found me wanting.'

He's getting good at this, thought Mark. 'What shifted the conversation?' he asked.

'When Michael stopped "controlling the message",' said Con, 'and just told us what actually happened.'

'That was important,' said Nicole, nodding at Michael. 'He had a choice at that point. I think I was angry because Michael hadn't trusted us. I assumed he didn't want to talk about it, that the subject was off limits. When he told us what happened, I began to question that assumption.'

'Great,' said Mark. 'Shall we talk about what other assumptions are supporting the dynamics of this team?'

Comings and goings

People join teams and people leave teams. When new people arrive and existing members leave, the dynamics of the team change. The container that has been built over time is disrupted. Some teams have rituals by which to welcome and farewell members. In other teams, entrances and departures are briefly attended to, or not attended to at all. If not attended to at all, then the container may stay disrupted. The team may try to carry on behaving the way it behaved before, without success. New patterns may emerge without being called out. Clashes may arise that weren't there before. New patterns of triangulation may appear, and so on and so on.

The way that teams manage entrances and exits reveals a lot about the dynamics of the team. What does it mean if no one says anything in the team forum, when someone leaves? What does it mean if no one says hello to the new arrival?

- Arrivals and departures are a great opportunity to learn about the dynamics of the team.
- Drawing attention to the impact of an arrival or departure enables teams to reflect on changes to team dynamics.
- Drawing attention to the impact of an arrival or departure further enables teams to assume responsibility for their team dynamics.

17 Patterns

In which the team start to manage their own dynamics

In the next two sessions, the team did some good work; in clarifying their collective purpose, agreeing some medium-term objectives, and working out how to better engage with the organisation as a whole. Michael played a proactive role in discussions, developing a good knack for managing the container. Sometimes he threw out a challenge to the team, other times he called out what was happening in the room. He pushed the pace on occasion and on other occasions supported others in setting the pace. Not everyone in the team displayed the same agility, and Mark decided it was time to introduce a language for helping the team work with patterns of dialogue.

Half way through the next session the team began talking about new market opportunities again, a subject that often resulted in them getting stuck. They got stuck again.

'I get so tired of this,' said Tim. 'Every time I bring up the subject, I seem to hit a brick wall.'

'I think it might be helpful to look at what just happened through a different lens,' said Mark. 'If you're all up for it?'

'We're up for it,' said Michael.

'Good. So, let me introduce you to a simple model,' said Mark. 'According to this model, anything anyone says is a vocal action that can be coded in one of four ways. The four vocal acts are Move, Follow, Oppose and Bystand.'

Mark pointed at Tim. 'Each time you invite the team to invest in new markets. That's a "Move". You're initiating movement. If instead of suggesting a Move yourself, you invited someone else to do so, that would still be a Move.'

'Got it,' said Tim.

'Each time someone challenges an idea, or offers a correction to someone else's move, that's an "Oppose".'

'I'm getting lots of Oppose,' muttered Tim darkly.

'Each time someone picks up on an idea in service of landing it, or making it happen, that's a "Follow". And when someone offers a perspective from outside or says what they are noticing in the conversation in a non-judgmental way, that's a "Bystand".'

People sat quietly, thinking.

'So what?' said Michael.

'So, it's a language that helps us notice when we get stuck and how we've become stuck. That enables us to come up with ways of getting unstuck.'

'For example?'

'For example, just now. What happened when Tim brought up the subject of new market opportunities?'

'He did a Move,' said Nicole.

'Yes,' said Mark. 'And what happened next?'

'Con rolled his eyes,' said Nicole. 'Elaine started talking about where we've got to in terms of lobbying the Government. Jo said the Board is waiting to see an investment case. Michael and I did some Bystanding.'

'OK,' said Mark. 'Let's break that down. Con rolled his eyes. So, Con, you are against the idea of investing in new markets?'

'I'm not against it,' said Con. 'I quite like the idea. I just know that we're not going to agree on anything and so it's a waste of time talking about it.'

'So, it looked like an Oppose,' said Mark. 'But when it comes to what Tim said, you are more inclined to Follow?'

'I guess,' said Con.

'Elaine. You then spoke about lobbying the Government. What was your intention? It sounded like a Bystand?'

'I'm opposed,' said Elaine. 'Now is not the time to be announcing new investment opportunities. Not while we're trying to persuade government to change their minds on the new regulations. They'll think we're awash with funds, and that will be that.'

'Thank you,' said Mark. 'Jo. The Board want to see an investment case. Is that miscellaneous information, or did you have some other intent?'

'It was a Follow!' said Jo. 'The Board are dying for us to put forward an investment case. It's all David ever talks about.'

'Thank you. And Michael and Nicole. Bystanding is a vocal act. If you're saying nothing, then we don't know what your intention is. That's not Bystanding, that's withdrawal.'

'Huh,' said Michael, frowning.

'So the first message I'd like to leave with you,' said Mark, 'is that one way for you to become more effective as a team is to work harder to make your intentions clear. So, for example, if you support something that someone else says, it might help to simply start with the words "I agree", or something like that.'

'I agree.' Michael nodded.

'The second message I'd like to leave with you is that when a team gets stuck, it's usually because one or other of the four action modes is missing. In this case Tim was providing a Move, Con seemed to be (and Elaine was) Opposing, and Jo seemed to be Bystanding. What was missing?'

'A clear Follow,' said Nicole. 'Even though Jo says she did a Follow, it wasn't apparent.'

'Great,' said Mark. 'What else?'

'Like what you're doing now,' said Michael. 'A Bystand on what's actually going on in the room.'

'Great.' Mark nodded. 'It may also help you, to understand which action modes you tend to go to first, or overuse. Understanding that often makes it more obvious that you may need to go outside your comfort zone, to be most useful in the moment.'

'I think Move for me,' said Tim, looking around. 'Jo's definitely a Bystander. She tends to just sit quietly, making the occasional observation. She even talks about the team sometimes as if she weren't a member of the team herself.'

'Elaine's good at challenging,' said Nicole. 'Which makes her strong in Oppose?'

They carried on a while, exploring the meaning of the four vocal acts and deciding how their individual preferences showed up in each other's behaviour.

'The point of the model,' said Mark, when they had finished, 'is to be able to reflect on when you get stuck. What's going on in terms of conversation patterns? And how might you get unstuck.'

'Right,' said Michael. 'Let's have the same conversation again, and this time I shall contribute.

'OK,' said Tim. 'I've half a mind to go back into "Move", but I'm not going to do that. Elaine. Tell us more as to why you seem so uncomfortable with my idea?'

The Four Player Model

David Kantor developed a series of models based on his observations of how families, and organisations, indeed any group of people, behaves. The Four Player Model suggests that everything we say can be categorised into one of four 'action modes'. When we '*Move*' we initiate something. For example, we propose a way forward, or invite someone else to suggest what to do next. When we '*Follow*' we support someone else's move, not just nodding silently, but validating the idea and moving it forward to completion. When we '*Oppose*' we challenge and correct the 'Move'. When we '*Bystand*' we provide a perspective on, for example, the content of the conversation, or the quality of the interaction. Either with reference to things that are going on outside the room, or with reference to the way the team is operating. The task of the facilitator is to help the team notice its own patterns of interaction using this language and equip them to be able to change the nature of their discourse, particularly when they get stuck in certain patterns.

When teams get stuck we can usually characterise that 'stuckness' with reference to the model. For example:

- When we see one member of the team Moving and all the others Following, all the time, we call this *courteous compliance*. Courteous compliance may look OK, but the team is unlikely to be very innovative, or responsive to scenarios outside the team leader's capability and experience. The challenge to the team is to liberate more Oppose, to access more Bystand, to enable an awareness of the stuck pattern itself.
- Sometimes we see *point-counterpoint*, a repetitive sequence of move-oppose-move-oppose. The team is stuck in monologue with team members focused only on advocating their own points of view, deaf to the views of others. The challenge here is to liberate the Follow, a collective commitment to exploring other people's perspectives, and again the Bystand, to draw attention to the nature of the stuckness.

Move   Follow   Oppose   Bystand

Figure 8 Four Player Model (after Kantor, 2012)

• In the *hall of mirrors*, every Move is followed by a series of Bystands. Ideas are offered up but no one follows through. When this happens, the team can break out of its stuckness by enabling more 'Follow', a commitment to building on ideas and working through how those ideas might be successfully implemented.

By drawing attention to patterns of dialogue, the facilitator can help teams develop the capacity to become unstuck, by themselves.

18 Breakthrough

In which the team goes forwards

'The reason I'm not comfortable with the idea,' replied Elaine, 'is that the message we've taken to Government so far, is that the regulatory changes they're proposing, will reduce our profitability to such a level that we won't be able to afford to invest in new infrastructure for several years. If it becomes known that we're about to make a new acquisition, our argument won't stand up.'

'In other words, we want the Government to think we're skint?' said Con.

'That can't be our objective,' said Nicole. 'As a publicly listed company, our financials are there for all to see. If they impose these changes on us then we will have to cut back on our investment plans, but we will still have money to invest.'

'We'll have to invest,' said Michael. 'To make back the shortfall in growth.'

'Can you tell us more about the message, Elaine,' said Jo. 'What exactly have we said so far?'

'We've said that these changes will make it harder for us to invest,' said Elaine. 'That's it so far. We will need to make our message more explicit as we move forward, but we haven't done so far. It's important to get the message right.'

'So, I'm hearing that if the changes go ahead,' Jo summarised, 'we will have less money to invest, but we will have to make some investments in order to make up the shortfall?'

Everyone nodded.

'So, this message needs to be very clear,' said Jo. 'because if we need to invest, we will need to start thinking about what those investments are now.'

'Actually, that's true,' said Michael, looking at Elaine.

'But we won't be investing in new infrastructure, in this country.' said Nicole. 'Isn't that the point?'

'I think so,' said Elaine, nodding. 'Which means I am less uncomfortable with Tim's desire to invest overseas, so long as the logic and the rationale are right.'

'Good,' said Michael. 'Which says we should start thinking about those new investments now.'

Tim smiled, Mark noticed, resisting the temptation to say 'Hallelujah!' he suspected.

'You're smiling, Tim,' he said.

'I am,' Tim replied. 'How easy was that? – is what I'm thinking. And all I did was ask Elaine to expand on her objection. Rather than engage in debate, which is what I've always done in the past, I just slowed myself down and asked a question. Then I didn't say anything else.'

'I reckon this could really work in our favour,' said Con, looking at Michael. 'You've always said you're uncomfortable making big acquisitions in overseas markets, where we have no track record, or understanding of the market. Well, what if we do overseas what our competitors are doing to us here? Forge partnerships with local marketing organisations, rather than seek to co-invest with the established infrastructure owners.' He looked at Tim. 'Leverage our marketing know-how.'

'And financial know-how,' said Nicole. 'One of the companies that advised us on the last acquisition specialises in that area.'

'I hadn't thought of that,' said Tim, with a glint in his eye.

'What a great message,' said Elaine, looking excited too. 'Impose regulation on us here, and we'll redirect our energies overseas. That's a real tender spot for the Government right now.'

Dialogue revisited

Mark was excited. For the first time in their working together, Michael and his team engaged easily in a dialogic process that led to a new outcome. Tim started it, by suspending his firmly held opinion that the business needed to invest in new market opportunities. He (authentically) expressed interest in Elaine's perspective. Con's Bystand then enabled Nicole to challenge what she understood Elaine to be saying, a challenge supported by Michael. To Elaine's credit, she didn't push back, but stayed in 'suspend'. Jo and Nicole navigated their understanding of what was being said carefully, inviting others to engage, a process that led to Elaine ultimately shifting her position.

When it became clear to Tim that the team was, for once, supporting his proposal to consider investing in new markets, he chose not to remind the team how many times they had engaged in the same conversation unsuccessfully. Instead he reflected publicly upon his own behaviour, and the contribution he made to shifting the group dynamic. Con, however, moved back into content, excited by some of the emerging possibilities. Nicole followed Con, creating a new vision of how they might all proceed, a variation on the original market investment idea, a version of investment that Tim acknowledged to be new.

It would be tempting to credit Con and Nicole with this breakthrough, but their contributions were made possible only by the engagement of everyone in dialogue. Everyone suspended whatever preconceptions they might have had about new investments, or in Con's case, about the team's capacity to engage in such a conversation successfully. No one came to the conversation with a pre-existing notion of what this market-entry might look like. That the team succeeded in coming up with something new, something co-created in the moment, is a sure sign that the team was engaged in dialogue. Note also, that this dialogue included people challenging each other. Nicole, for example, pushed back on Elaine. She did so respectfully however, in a way that Elaine was happy to support.

Well done team.

1 Retrenchment

In which the team goes backwards

The next couple of sessions went well too. The team found the Four Player Model useful, and both Tim and Elaine seemed newly energised, relieved that this new model seemed to validate both their preferred styles. Things definitely seemed to be progressing. The team also talked about how to better engage the Board, getting clarity around their mandate in terms of coming up with a revised strategy. As part of that conversation the team openly challenged Jo on her behaviour within the team, which Jo responded to calmly and thoughtfully.

There was a new momentum in the team, and so it took Mark by surprise when the next meeting started badly. Michael was in a bad mood, Tim was quiet, and Elaine and Nicole weren't talking to each other. The check-in was quick and perfunctory.

'What's going on?' asked Mark.

'We haven't had a good week,' said Michael. 'I lost my temper with Tim, and Elaine and Nicole fell out over … well, I'll let them tell you what they fell out over.'

Elaine sat with arms crossed and mouth firmly closed. Nicole played with her pen.

'How about we try and talk about what happened without getting into content?' said Mark. 'How about talking about it from the perspective of dialogue? How did you go in engaging in dialogue with each other? What did you notice about some of the patterns?'

'I totally failed,' said Michael. 'Tim collared me yesterday morning, evidently excited, and started taking me through a particular alliance he's been working on. I'd just had a difficult meeting with one of the Board members who took me to task for not being faster off the mark with a response to the new legislation. I wasn't in the right frame of mind and told Tim everything that was wrong with his idea.' He waved a hand. 'Which might be a great idea, I don't know, but I just was listening. Sorry Tim.'

Tim nodded, but said nothing.

'Elaine's cross with Nicole because Nicole said she didn't think ts stuff around "controlling the message" makes sense,' said Con. 'Nicc said that you need to engage people in open consultation if you rea want them on your side. They had an argument in front of the rest of i. It really got quite heated.' He sat back in his chair and grinned.

'Makes me wonder what it's all been for,' said Michael, desponde. 'Seems like we're back where we started.'

'In what sense?' asked Mark.

'Same old tensions, same old issues,' said Michael. 'Same old n-dency to fly off the handle. Me anyway.'

'I don't think we're back where we started,' said Jo. 'Far from it.Ve can talk about what happened now in ways we couldn't before. On may be revelling in the chaos right now, but his analysis seems broaly correct to me. It's been a hard week for everyone and we haven't ten at our best.' She turned to Elaine and Nicole. 'You're both right. Wdo need to be thoughtful about the messages we put out there, and we red to listen to what others are saying and thinking. We need to leveige both perspectives.'

'Yes,' said Nicole. 'I agree. I shouldn't have got into an argument ith you Elaine. I should have put more energy into understanding were you were coming from.'

'OK,' said Elaine, uncrossing her arms. 'I should have done the sane.'

'And let's not fall into the trap of making this just about you wo,' said Jo. 'We are supposed to be a team, as I have been reminded recatly. Any one of the rest of us might have intervened, tried to take us ito a more reflective space, but none of us did that.'

'So, you retrenched,' said Mark. 'It's a natural part of this worl. It's absolutely to be expected. Change isn't linear. There will always be imes when you revert back to old, familiar, patterns of behaviour.'

'How do we manage it moving forward?' asked Michael.

'I think you know the answer to that,' said Mark, looking at Jo. 'When you move into a way of behaving that isn't where you want to be, then it's because something is triggering that pattern. You're falling back into old patterns for a reason. That's nothing to beat yourselves up about. Instead, make the space to reflect on it, as Jo said. Take the opportunity to learn about the dynamic of the team. In the long run that will make you even more capable of managing those dynamics when you need to.'

'Makes sense,' said Michael. 'Let's use this time then to reflect on yesterday. How about we start with you, Con. You seemed to have enjoyed it more than anyone?'

20 Exiting the container

In which the team checks out

'Before we close,' said Mark. 'I'd like us all to think carefully about how we check out today. I've noticed the last couple of times we've met, that people have said things like "it was good" and "I think we did well", I'd like to talk a little bit about that.'

'You mean people aren't saying what they really think?' said Michael.

'Not necessarily,' said Mark. 'People often do use phrases like that instead of saying what they're really thinking, and that's something to watch out for and be curious about. But what I'd like to do though, is talk about the check-out again in the context of the "container".'

'You mean the safe space, the trust …'

'I do,' said Mark. 'I wouldn't want you to think of dialogue as some sort of religious ritual.' He waved a hand at the others in the circle. 'When people sit in the circle with no table etc …, people do sometimes think they have to behave a certain way until the circle is broken again. Remember, we said you can't make dialogue happen, you can only create conditions under which it might happen. And while you're in the circle you'll find yourselves moving in and out of dialogue, and that's fine too.'

'And that links with the check-out how?' asked Michael.

'Think about today's session,' said Mark. 'Think about how it started and where it went. Think about Jo's comments about reflection. The check-out is a wonderful opportunity to engage in some of that reflection. What was your experience of the meeting today? What emerged that you haven't seen before? What have you learned together? Spend some time really thinking about the answer to some of these questions, in service of continually improving and getting better at being a team.'

'I'll go first,' said Con. 'I'm feeling guilty. A couple of people called out that I enjoyed some of the stress that people went through yesterday. Truth is, I think I did a bit. I recognise that I'm still carrying some frustration and resentment around with me, about the way the acquisition was managed. A lot of the people who I knew and worked with before the take-over, have been stressed ever since coming over. I think I've only realised today that I really haven't ever been fully committed to this team. I need to think on that one some more.'

'Heavy stuff,' said Tim in admiration. 'Thanks for sharing that, Con. I, for one, really appreciate it. What I'd like to share with everyone is that I'm feeling encouraged as to how we made sense of what happened the last two days. I'm leaving this conversation with an experience of having sorted some stuff out and moved on.'

'Me too,' said Jo. 'I've also realised that I'm pretty high in "Bystand". I think I'd like to keep leveraging that for the sake of the team, as well as taking more responsibility for making suggestions as to how we can do things better, in particular when it comes to influencing the Board.'

'I'm beginning to see myself as some of you maybe see me,' said Elaine, without smiling. 'I'm not always good at taking feedback, but I want to get better. I hope you'll give me honest feedback if I ask for it, and I plan to make more of an effort to listen to others.'

'I like working in this team,' said Nicole. 'That's my biggest take-away from today. I don't know that I could have honestly said that a few months ago. We have a big challenge ahead of us, but I'm beginning to get excited about what we might achieve together.'

'Thanks everyone,' said Michael. 'I'm really encouraged to hear you all speak. I share those views. One of the things that's been on my mind, as you know, is who we ask to step up and replace Karen. I know in the past I would have asked you your opinions, but I would have made my mind up already. This time I plan to talk to all of you, and I promise you I don't have a fixed view, and I really want to hear what you all have to say.' He looked across the room. 'That includes you, Tim.'

'Just you left,' said Con, looking to Mark.

'I'm just sitting here in awe,' said Mark. 'So many great insights, so many learnings. I sense you all becoming masters of your own container and I sense a real transformation in you all as a team.'

Working with the team – summary

The diagram below summarises the journey that Michael and Mark embarked upon with the rest of Michael's team. The container metaphor is a great one for capturing the work involved in enabling dialogue to take place within a team, or indeed any group of people. As we saw, Mark did quite a lot of work before attempting to engage the team in dialogue. He worked closely with Hannah and then contracted with Michael to ensure they both aligned around the purpose for dialogue. They also made sure they agreed on the roles they would each play. He spoke to team members and prepared himself for stepping into the container. He thought about the setting, an environment in which the team had the best chance of engaging in dialogue.

Once in the room with the team, Mark made decisions based on his sense of the state of the container. In the early sessions, he focused on building the container, facilitating the emergence of trust and curiosity. He helped the group define a purpose for dialogue, and encouraged them to listen, voice and reflect aloud. Once he judged the container was ready, he introduced perturbance, or worked with the perturbance that was already there, like when Karen left the team. He worked with patterns of dialogue, helping the team assume responsibility for managing the container themselves, by introducing them to a new language.

Finally, when the time was right, he invited them to reflect upon what they had learned from being in dialogue. He encouraged them to continue to engage in dialogue especially when facing complex change. The challenge for them now was to integrate dialogue into the way they worked together, long term.

Some of the tools and theories Mark accessed, including triangulation, and the Four Player Model, are just Mark's favourites.

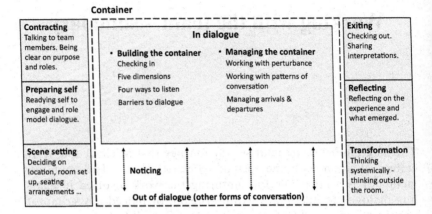

Figure 9 Beanacre Model

There are many different approaches he could have used, and we've used these only to illustrate how he worked more broadly within the overall framework. Working with dialogue is a wonderfully innovative and creative process!

Part III

Michael, Mark and Hannah

21 Reflection

In which Michael, Mark and Hannah reflect on what the team achieved

Michael invited Mark and Hannah out for lunch.

'I want to thank you for the work you've done so far, Mark,' said Michael. 'What I'd like to do over lunch is reflect on what the team has achieved, and how that links into the original agenda which was all about dialogue.'

'What are your reflections?' asked Hannah.

'Mmm,' said Michael. 'Well, in the work you and I did together, Hannah, I thought I understood what dialogue was and how to do it. I thought about it in terms of listening in a particular way and having the courage to speak my mind. I thought that the work we did as a team would just be about teaching everyone else on the team the same lessons, then getting on with it.'

'And now?'

'Now ...' Michael pondered. 'That's still how I see dialogue, but I get the point of this "container" business, creating a space in which people feel comfortable engaging in dialogue. It's much more complex when you have a bunch of people in the room. I've learned a few things from Mark about how I can do that myself.'

'Great!' said Mark. 'I've seen you doing it a fair bit recently.'

'Yes, and I've had my not-so-wonderful moments too, but I like the idea that dialogue is dynamic and sometimes fleeting. That doesn't just make me feel better, it feels real. I like the idea that we can check-in all the time, not just at the beginning and end of a conversation, to see how we're doing, and that sometimes we'll find we've been in dialogue, sometimes we won't. Sometimes we'll find that a few of us have been trying to get us into dialogue and others have been disengaged, so it hasn't worked in the way we might have hoped for. It feels like I have an understanding now as to how we can create that ... what to call it ... magic?'

He looked to Mark and Hannah to see if they'd laugh. 'Didn't think I'd hear myself saying that, but that's what it's felt like sometimes. Like the time when Con confessed to feeling guilty. Like the time we worked through Karen's departure from the team, like the way Jo took all that stuff on the chin about being an outsider.'

'Any other reflections?' said Hannah.

'The idea that you can turn up the heat and turn it back down again in really productive and generative ways,' said Michael. 'I think I'd always thought before that you need to keep the heat down as low as it will go to contain everything.' He looked at Mark. 'And of course, the language we can use to notice patterns of dialogue, and how personal the language is that we use. I see all of that. I just have one question I think. For you, Hannah.'

'Shoot,' said Hannah.

'We talked about me and we talked about the organisation. We said that my team was the place to start in terms of seeking to change the organisation. My question is, what next? How do we take this "dialogic mindset" out to the whole company?'

'Good question,' said Hannah. 'I would like to come back, Michael,' she said. 'I would like to be your Head of Organisational Development, reporting directly to you. My role will be to build on what you, as the CEO, have been doing differently, and to build on what the executive team have been doing in learning how to engage in collective dialogue. Now is the right time to begin to engage the whole organisation in dialogue. We can't expect everyone to be in dialogue all the time. Nor would that necessarily be useful. But we do need to work out who *does* need to engage in dialogue with who, and when. That will require a dialogic and systemic approach to building the capability of this organisation.'

Michael nodded thoughtfully. 'Makes sense to me, Hannah. But I want to engage in some dialogue with the rest of the leadership team first. They may have some perspectives that I haven't thought of, that I'm not aware of. Is that OK with you?'

'Yes,' said Hannah, smiling. 'That's fine.'

Bibliography

Beech, N., Kajzer-Mitchell, I., Oswick, C. & Saren, M. (2011) Barriers to change and identity work in the swampy lowland. *Journal of Change Management*, 11(3), 289–304.

Bohm, D. (1992) *Thought as a System*. London: Routledge.

Bohm, D. (1996) *On Dialogue*. London: Routledge.

Bohm, D. (1996) *On Creativity*. London: Routledge.

Bond, C. & Seneque, M. (2012) Exploring organizational identity in the context of transformational change: A South African case study. *Journal of Change Management*, 12(1), 13–30.

Bowen, M. (1993) *Family Therapy in Clinical Practice*. Lanham, MA: Jason Aronson.

Buchanan, D. A. & Badham, R. J. (2008) *Power, Politics, and Organizational Change: Winning the Turf Game*. London: Sage.

Burnes, B. (2004) Kurt Lewin and complexity theories: Back to the future? *Journal of Change Management*, 4(4), 309–325.

Burnes, B. (2011) Introduction: Why does change fail, and what can we do about it? *Journal of Change Management*, 11(4), 445–450.

Burnes, B. & Jackson, P. (2011) Success and failure in organizational change: An exploration of the role of values. *Journal of Change Management*, 11(2), 133–162.

Bushe, G. & Marshak, R. (2015) *Dialogic Organization Development: The Theory and Practice of Transformational Change*. Oakland, CA: Berrett-Koehler.

Caldwell, S. (2013) Are change readiness strategies overrated? A commentary on boundary conditions. *Journal of Change Management*, 13(1), 19–35.

Charles, K. & Dawson, P. (2011) Dispersed change agency and the improvisation of strategies during processes of change. *Journal of Change Management*, 11(3), 329–351.

Conway, E. & Monks, K. (2011) Change from below: The role of middle managers in mediating paradoxical change. *Human Resource Management Journal*, 21(2), 190–203.

Cooperrider, D., Sorensen, P., Whitney, D. & Yaeger, T. (2000) *Appreciative Inquiry – Rethinking human organisation toward a positive theory of change*. Champaigne, IL: Stipes Publishing.

van Dijk, R. & Van Dick, R. (2009) Navigating organizational change: Change leaders, employee resistance and work-based identities. *Journal of Change Management*, 9(2), 143–163.

Ford, R. (2008) Complex adaptive systems and improvisation theory: Toward framing a model to enable continuous change. *Journal of Change Management*, 8(3–4), 173–198.

Ford, J. D. & Ford, L. W. (1995) The role of conversations in producing intentional change in organizations. *Academy of Management Review*, 20(3), 541–570.

Ford, J. D., Ford, L. W. & D'Amelio, A. (2008) Resistance to change: The rest of the story. *Academy of Management Review*, 33(2), 362–377.

Gilley, A., McMillan, H. S. & Gilley, J. W. (2009) Organizational change and characteristics of leadership effectiveness. *Journal of Leadership & Organizational Studies*, 16(1), 38–47.

Gover, L. & Duxbury, L. (2012) Organizational faultlines: Social identity dynamics and organizational change. *Journal of Change Management*, 12(1), 53–75.

Graetz, F. & Smith, A. C. T. (2010) Managing organizational change: A philosophies of change approach. *Journal of Change Management*, 10(2), 135–154.

Grant, D. & Marshak, R. J. (2011) Toward a discourse-centered understanding of organizational change. *The Journal of Applied Behavioral Science*, 47(2), 204–235.

Hardy, C. & Phillips, N. (2004) Discourse and power. In D. Grant, C. Hardy, C. Oswick & L. Putnam (Eds.), *The Sage Handbook of Organizational Discourse* (pp. 299–316). London: Sage.

Higgs, M. & Rowland, D. (2005) All changes great and small: Exploring approaches to change and its leadership. *Journal of Change Management*, 5(2), 121–151.

Higgs, M. & Rowland, D. (2011) What does it take to implement change successfully? A study of the behaviors of successful change leaders. *The Journal of Applied Behavioral Science*, 47(3), 309–335.

Hill, S., Hare, U. & Ball, J. (2004) 'We've all come together as one – prisoners, staff and managers': Prison Dialogue as a means of facilitating patient/public involvement and implementing new standards in prison healthcare. *Prison Service Journal*, 151, 30–35.

Hill, S. (2017) *Where Did You Learn To Behave Like That? A Coaching Guide for Working with Leader*. London: Dialogix Ltd, Createspace Publishing.

Hughes, M. (2011) Do 70 per cent of all organizational change initiatives really fail? *Journal of Change Management*, 11(4), 451–464.

Isaacs, W. (1999) *Dialogue and the Art of Thinking Together*. New York: Doubleday

Jabri, M., Adrian, A. D. & Boje, D. (2008) Reconsidering the role of conversations in change communication: A contribution based on Bakhtin. *Journal of Organizational Change Management*, 21(6), 667–685.

Jaworski, J. (1998) *Synchronicity – The Inner Path of Leadership*. Oakland, CA: Berrett-Koehler.

Johansson, C. & Heide, M. (2008) Speaking of change: Three communication approaches in studies of organizational change. *Corporate Communications: An International Journal*, 13(3), 288–305.

Judge, W. & Douglas, T. (2009) Organizational change capacity: The systematic development of a scale. *Journal of Organizational Change Management*, 22(6), 635–649.

Kantor, D. (2012) *Reading the Room*. San Francisco, CA: Jossey-Bass.

Kahane, A. (2004) *Solving Tough Problems: An Open Way of Talking, Listening, and Creating New Realities*. San Francisco, CA: Berrett-Koehler.

Kahane, A. (2010) *Power and Love: A Theory and Practice of Social Change*. San Francisco, CA: Berrett-Koehler.

Krishnamurti, J. (1968) *Talks and Dialogues*. New York: Avon Books.

Landsberg, M. (2015) *The Tao of Coaching: Boost Your Effectiveness at Work by Inspiring and Developing Those Around You*. London: Profile Books.

Lawrence, P. (2014) *Leading Change: How Successful Leaders Approach Change Management*. London: Kogan Page.

Lawrence, P. (2015) Leading Change – Insights Into How Leaders Actually Approach the Challenge of Complexity. *Journal of Change Management*, 15(3), 231–252.

Lawrence, P. & Moore, A. (2018) *Coaching in Three Dimensions. Meeting the Challenges of a Complex World*. UK: Routledge.

Lewin, K. (1958) Group decision and social change. In E. E. Maccoby, T. M. Newcomb & E. L. Hartley (Eds.), *Readings in social psychology* (pp. 197–211). Holt, NY: Rinehart and Winston.

Marshak, R. M. & Grant, D. (2008) Organizational discourse and new organization development practices. *British Journal of Management*, 19, S7–S19.

McClellan, J. (2011) Reconsidering communication and the discursive politics of organizational change. *Journal of Change Management*, 11(4), 465–480.

Mindell, A. (1995) *Sitting in the Fire*. Portland, OR: Lao Tse Press,

van Nistelrooij, A. & Sminia, H. (2010) Organization development: What's actually happening? Journal of Change Management, 10(4), 407–420.

Raelin, J. D. & Cataldo, C. G. (2011) Whither middle management? Empowering interface and the failure of organizational change. *Journal of Change Management*, 11(4), 481–507.

Ray, K. W. & Goppelt, J. (2011) Understanding the effects of leadership development on the creation of organizational culture change: A research approach. *International Journal of Training and Development*, 15(1), 58–75.

Reissner, S. C. (2010) Change, meaning and identity at the workplace. *Journal of Organizational Change Management*, 23(3), 287–299.

Salem, P. (2008) The seven communication reasons organizations do not change. *Corporate Communications: An International Journal*, 13(3), 333–348.

Schein, E. H. (1988) *Process consultation: Its role in organization development*. Reading, MA: Addison-Wesley.

Senge, P., Kleiner, A., Roberts, C., Ross, R. & Smith, B. (1994) *The Fifth Discipline Fieldbook: Strategies for Building a Learning Organisation*. New York: Nicholas Brealey Publishing.

Senge, P. et al. (2004) *Presence*. Boston, MA: Nicholas Brealey Publishing.

Shaw, P. (1997) Intervening in the shadow systems of organizations: consulting from a complexity perspective. *Journal of Organizational Change Management*, 10(3), 235–250.

Shaw, P. (2002) *Changing Conversations in Organisations*. London: Routledge.

Stacey, R. (1996) *Complexity and Creativity in Organizations*. San Francisco, CA: Berrett-Koehler.

Stacey, R. (2012) *Tools and Techniques of Leadership and Management. Meeting the challenge of complexity*. London: Routledge.

Thomas, R. & Hardy, C. (2011) Reframing resistance to organizational change. *Scandinavian Journal of Management*, 27, 322–331.

Thurlow, A. & Helms Mills, J. (2009) Change, talk and sensemaking. *Journal of Organizational Change Management*, 22(5), 459–479.

Tsoukas, H. & Chia, R. (2002) On organizational becoming: Rethinking organizational change. *Organization Science*, 13(5), 567–582.

Tsoukas, H. & Hatch, M. J. (2001) Complex thinking, complex practice: The case for a narrative approach to organizational complexity. *Human Relations*, 54(8), 979–1013.

van de Ven, A. H. & Sun, K. (2011) Breakdowns in implementing models of organization change. *Academy of Management Perspectives*, 25(3), 58–74.

Weick, K. E., Sutcliffe, K. M. & Obstfeld, D. (2005) Organizing and the process of sensemaking. *Organization Science*, 16(4), 409–421.

Werkman, R. (2010) Reinventing organization development: How a sensemaking perspective can enrich OD theories and interventions. *Journal of Change Management*, 10(4), 421–438.

Wheatley, M. (2002) *Turning to One Another*. Oakland, CA: Berrett-Koehler.

Wheatley, M. (2004) *Finding our Way*. Oakland, CA: Berrett-Koehler.

Wheatley, M. & Kellner-Rogers, M. (1998) *A Simpler Way*. Oakland, CA: Berrett-Koehler.

Index